Protestants in America

UNION HILL BAPTIST CHURCH

JON BUTLER & HARRY S. STOUT
GENERAL EDITORS

Protestants in America

Mark A. Noll

To Robert, of course

OXFORD
UNIVERSITY PRESS

Oxford New York
Athens Auckland Bangkok Bogotá Buenos Aires Calcutta
Cape Town Chennai Dar es Salaam Delhi Florence Hong Kong Istanbul
Karachi Kuala Lumpur Madrid Melbourne Mexico City Mumbai
Nairobi Paris São Paulo Singapore Taipei Tokyo Toronto Warsaw
and associated companies in
Berlin Ibadan

Published by Oxford University Press, Inc.
198 Madison Avenue, New York, New York 10016
www.oup.com

Library of Congress Cataloging-in-Publication Data

Noll, Mark A.
Protestants in America / by Mark A. Noll; general editors, Jon Butler and Harry S. Stout.
p. cm. — (Religion in American life) Includes bibliographical references and index.
Summary: Discusses the origins of Protestantism, the diversity of Protestant churches in the United States, and the role of Protestants from colonial times to the present.
ISBN 0-19-511034-X (library edition)
1. Protestant churches-United States-History-Juvenile literature. [1. Protestant churches-History.] I. Butler, Jon, 1940- II. Stout, Harry S. III. Title. IV. Series.

BR515 .N745 2000
280'.4'0973-dc21 00-027271

9 8 7 6 5 4 3 2 1

Printed in the United States of America
on acid-free paper

Design and layout: Loraine Machlin
Picture research: Lisa Kirchner

On the cover: Camp Meeting of the Methodists in North America, 1819, by M. Dubourg (engraver) and Jacques Gérard Milbert (painter).

Frontispiece: Dinner on the grounds of the Union Hill Baptist Church in Nashville in the 1950s.

Contents

FAITH
LIFE
UNITY
APOSTOLIC

Editors' Introduction

JON BUTLER & HARRY S. STOUT, GENERAL EDITORS

Since the earliest European settlers reached the shores of Massachusetts and Virginia in the 17th century, Protestantism has been inextricably linked with the development of American politics and culture. Fervent beliefs about Scripture, morality, and the force of faith have driven Protestants throughout American history to exercise great influence in public life, from meeting houses and school houses to the White House.

In *Protestants in America,* Mark Noll emphasizes the staggering variety of the Protestant experience in America. Tracing a history that includes several waves of development, Noll explores the tremendous diversity found in the myriad denominations we label "Protestant." From the early Puritans who wanted to build "a city on a hill" for God to the recent flourishing of African-American, Hispanic, and Asian-American Protestant churches, that diversity is filled with lively contradiction. Noll explains how Phoebe Worrall Palmer quoted Scripture to support women leaders in the church while her opponents did the same to keep them out; how Martin Luther King, Jr., and his Southern Christian Leadership Conference found strength in a faith that slaveholders had once used to justify chattel slavery; and how Protestant adaptability has moved the religion from colonial Puritanism to televangelism and suburban "megachurches" in the early 21st century. From John Winthrop, Anne Hutchinson, and

Charles F. Parham (front, left) with a group of Christian workers in front of the courthouse in Carthage, Missouri, in 1905. Parham, a Holiness preacher who stressed the gifts of the Holy Spirit, opened schools and conducted meetings throughout Missouri and Kansas.

Harriet Beecher Stowe to the Salvation Army, the Women's Christian Temperance Union, Billy Graham, and President Jimmy Carter—here are the individuals and institutions that have shaped a religious presence so similar, so diverse, and so formidable that we cannot imagine America without it.

This book is part of a unique 17-volume series that explores the evolution, character, and dynamics of religion in American life from 1500 to the end of the 20th century. As late as the 1960s, historians paid relatively little attention to religion beyond studies of New England's Puritans. But since then, American religious history and its contemporary expression have been the subject of intense inquiry. These new studies have thoroughly transformed our knowledge of almost every American religious group and have fully revised our understanding of religion's role in U.S. history.

It is impossible to capture the flavor and character of the American experience without understanding the connections between secular activities and religion. Spirituality stood at the center of Native American societies before European colonization and has continued to do so long after. Religion—and the freedom to express it—motivated millions of immigrants to come to the United States from remarkably different cultures, and the exposure to new ideas and ways of living shaped their experience. It also fueled tension among different ethnic and racial groups in America and, regretfully, accounted for difficult episodes of bigotry in American society. Religion urged Americans to expand the nation—first within the continental United States, then through overseas conquests and missionary work—and has had a profound influence on American politics, from the era of the Puritans to the present. Finally, religion contributes to the extraordinary diversity that has, for four centuries, made the United States one of the world's most dynamic societies.

The Religion in American Life series explores the historical traditions that have made religious freedom and spiritual exploration central features of American society. It emphasizes the experience of religion in America—what men and women have understood by religion, how it has affected politics and society, and how Americans have used it to shape their daily lives.

JON BUTLER & HARRY S. STOUT
GENERAL EDITORS

RELIGION IN COLONIAL AMERICA
Jon Butler

RELIGION IN NINETEENTH CENTURY AMERICA
Grant Wacker

RELIGION IN TWENTIETH CENTURY AMERICA
Randall Balmer

BUDDHISTS, HINDUS, AND SIKHS IN AMERICA
Gurinder Singh Mann, Paul David Numrich & Raymond B. Williams

CATHOLICS IN AMERICA
James T. Fisher

JEWS IN AMERICA
Hasia R. Diner

MORMONS IN AMERICA
Claudia Lauper Bushman & Richard Lyman Bushman

MUSLIMS IN AMERICA
Frederick Denny

ORTHODOX CHRISTIANS IN AMERICA
John H. Erickson

PROTESTANTS IN AMERICA
Mark A. Noll

AFRICAN-AMERICAN RELIGION
Albert J. Raboteau

ALTERNATIVE AMERICAN RELIGIONS
Stephen J. Stein

CHURCH AND STATE IN AMERICA
Edwin S. Gaustad

IMMIGRATION AND AMERICAN RELIGION
Jenna Weissman Joselit

NATIVE AMERICAN RELIGION
Joel W. Martin

WOMEN AND AMERICAN RELIGION
Ann Braude

BIOGRAPHICAL SUPPLEMENT AND SERIES INDEX
Darryl Hart & Ann Henderson Hart

Chapter 1

Who are the Protestants?

The day was August 28, 1963. The place was the Mall in Washington, D.C. More than 200,000 people were gathered in the shadow of the Lincoln Memorial, almost exactly 100 years after Abraham Lincoln had issued the Emancipation Proclamation that freed the slaves in the states of the Confederacy. They were there for a "March on Washington" to promote the civil rights of African Americans. After a full day of speeches, one more speaker came to the microphone: the Rev. Martin Luther King, Jr. King had vaulted into national prominence less than a decade earlier when he led a boycott of the buses in Montgomery, Alabama. As in much of the South, blacks were not allowed to sit in the front seats no matter how jammed the rear sections designated for them were or how empty the designated "white" sections in the front. In 1957 King had helped organize the Southern Christian Leadership Conference (SCLC), whose goal was to promote civil rights for all Americans.

As King began to speak, he first referred to the Emancipation Proclamation. Then he detailed the ways in which "the Negro is still not free." Next he outlined the goals and programs of the civil rights movement. And then he began one of the most moving conclusions of any public address in U. S. history by proclaiming, "I have a dream today." The dream was of an America where skin color was no longer a badge of honor or a mark of dishonor. It was a dream of a nation where, quoting an African-American spiritual, King hoped that everyone would one day be "Free at last."

The Southern Baptist Convention is the largest Protestant denomination in the United States, with nearly 16 million members as of 1999. In recent years it has become a more ethnically diverse church, with particularly rapid growth in its Spanish-speaking congregations.

Just before he said these words, King declared that in his dream "every valley shall be exalted, every hill and mountain shall be made low. The rough places will be plain and the crooked places will be made straight, and the glory of the Lord shall be revealed, and all flesh shall see it together." These words come from the 40th chapter of the book of Isaiah in the Old Testament of the Bible. King's message about civil rights was a Protestant message. To be sure, it was not the only view held by American Protestants on the subject. In fact, some other Protestants were among King's fiercest opponents in the civil rights struggle. Yet King's use of the Christian Scriptures to make a point in public, as well as his desire to apply religious ideals to the shaping of American society, were characteristics that have always marked Protestant life in American history.

King was a minister at different times in two of the largest African-American Baptist denominations, the National Baptist Convention,

Martin Luther King, Jr.'s leadership in the civil rights movement of the 1960s made him the best-known American clergyman of his era.

U.S.A., Inc., and the Progressive National Baptist Convention. Another modern American Protestant, Billy Graham, is also a member of a Baptist denomination, the Southern Baptist Convention. Billy Graham is known worldwide as an evangelist, someone who preaches the Christian "gospel," a word which comes from the Greek for "good news" in the New Testament. In his "crusades for Christ," Billy Graham has spoken to more people in public meetings than any other figure in Protestant history. Hundreds of millions more have seen him on television or read his books.

Billy Graham in a publicity photo from 1940, in front of a cross with JESUS SAVES written on it. Graham later carried his Bible-centered message around the world.

The main themes of Graham's career are as common to American Protestant history as King's were. Graham, like King, was raised in a religious home. In 1944 he became the first full-time employee of Youth for Christ, International, one of several missionary movements founded by Protestants during and immediately after World War II. In 1949, Graham and his associates planned a three-week series of meetings in Los Angeles. They rented a large tent, as generations of Protestant preachers had done before. This gathering in Los Angeles, however, became something quite out of the ordinary. A number of famous individuals—athletes, mobsters, and Hollywood celebrities—responded to Graham's appeal. They "surrendered their lives to Jesus Christ," a phrase that had been heard with many variations from many Protestant preachers in American history. Near the end of the three weeks, newspaper mogul William Randolph Hearst heard about the event and ordered his papers to promote the young evangelist. Almost instantly, Billy Graham became a celebrity. The Los Angeles meetings were extended and many more people "came to Christ." These events launched Graham on a highly visible public career that has lasted for half a century.

Billy Graham's depiction of the relationship between God and humanity has not been shared by all Protestants. In fact, some Protestants have written off Graham as a "fundamentalist" reactionary out of touch with modern times. Still others have condemned him as a rank "modernist" who is far too friendly with far too many people who do not toe the straight and narrow line defined by self-described "fundamentalists." (Although the word is used more generally now, "fundamentalists" originally meant practitioners of revivalistic Protestantism who opposed modern alterations in Christian theology. "Modernists," by contrast, were those who welcomed these changes, such as the idea that Jesus' resurrection from the dead was spiritual rather than literal.) Yet Billy Graham's type of evangelistic preaching from the Bible and his lifelong emphasis on the "new birth" have been themes prominent from the very first days of Protestantism in America.

Who are the Protestants? The question is more difficult than it first appears. Martin Luther King, Jr., and Billy Graham are Protestants, but so are some of their most strenuous critics.

Some Protestants worship God in large, expensive churches designed by well-paid architects. Others worship God in their living rooms, in storefronts, or in nondescript structures with no aesthetic appeal at all.

Some Protestants pray to God with carefully written prayers, often of ancient origin. Others pray while "speaking in tongues"—ecstatic speech that believers feel is given to them by the Holy Spirit. Most Protestants pray by mixing spontaneity and formula, usually not writing out prayers but often employing figures of speech, set phrases, and rhythmic patterns common to their own groups.

Some Protestants sing hymns written by their forefathers (and foremothers), some sing songs written much more recently. Some Protestant hymns combine deep emotion and substantial theological content, like one written by Samuel Davies, an early Protestant minister in Virginia, from the 1750s:

> Pardon from an offended God!
> Pardon for sins of deepest dye!
> Pardon bestowed through Jesus' blood!
> Pardon that brings the rebel nigh!
> Who is a pard'ning God like thee?
> Or who has grace so rich and free?

This down-home structure is a building like many of the humble places used for worship by Protestants throughout American history.

Many Protestant hymns evoke religious feeling by appealing to domestic themes. In the second half of the 19th century, there was a flourishing of the "gospel song," which often employed biblical images with straightforward tunes aimed right at the person in the street.

For some Protestants, music is a high art defined by classical composers like Johann Sebastian Bach. For others it is a folk art defined by the African-American spiritual or by troubadours of the people.

A few Protestants have been in the forefront of American intellectual life. More have been suspicious of formal learning as a threat to genuine faith. Most have promoted learning as a helpful, though not all-important, activity.

Some Protestants have supported politically radical causes, like the American Revolution in the 18th century, the campaign against liquor in the 19th and early 20th centuries, or the rights of labor unions in the early days of industrialization. Other Protestants have been political conservatives, like enemies of President Thomas Jefferson in the early 1800s (who thought he was too fond of "atheistic France"), or opponents of woman suffrage in the 19th century (who thought giving women the vote would undermine their care of the home), or supporters of President Woodrow Wilson in World War I (who thought that backing the war would advance Christian civilization worldwide). Many Protestants have been relatively nonpolitical, because they think that spiritual realities are more important than participation in public life.

Some Protestants, who trace their origins to the European continent, belong to churches called Lutheran, Reformed, Mennonite, Moravian, and Brethren. Others, with roots in the British Isles, are known as Episcopalians, Presbyterians, Baptists, Methodists, Congregationalists, or Salvationists (of the Salvation Army). Still others are associated with churches or denominations that took shape in America itself, such as the Churches of Christ, Christian Churches, Disciples of Christ, Seventh-day Adventists, the Church of the Nazarene, and Pentecostal denominations such as the Assemblies of God or the Church of God in Christ. Many other Protestants belong to independent congregations that are not attached to denominations. These churches sometimes have distinctive, biblical-sounding names: "Maranatha Christian Revival Center," "House the Lord Built Fellowship Church," "Christian Temple of the Revelation," or "Upon this Rock Christian Center." Other independent congregations are called "Bible Churches," "Community Fellowships," and similarly generic names. Still other Protestants meet in homes in groups that may not be named at all.

The ethnic origins of American Protestants are almost as diverse as their denominations. Many Protestant churches have their origin in England, Scotland, Wales, or Ireland. Still others are connected historically to Germany, Scandinavia, or the Netherlands. A few have ties to France, Italy, and Eastern Europe. African-American churches constitute a large and diverse range of Protestants. In the second half of the 20th century, the number of Hispanic and Asian-American Protestants has risen much more rapidly than the population at large. And many Protestant churches are simply "American" without any discernable foreign connections.

It should be obvious from this extensive—but incomplete—list of differences why it is so difficult to answer the question, "Who are the Protestants?" Well-known individuals like Martin Luther King, Jr., and Billy

Graham illustrate some of the traits that have been prominent in Protestant history, but by no means all. It is a basic reality that Protestants have no single structure and no single spokesperson. Many powerful Protestant leaders throughout the years have been called the "pope" of this or that region or denomination. But that designation is only a metaphor, since Protestants as a whole have never possessed the type of administrative structure that for Roman Catholics culminates in the pope.

Taking a brief look at three noteworthy figures from early American history will illustrate Protestant diversity, but also show some connections with the lives of Martin Luther King, Jr., and Billy Graham.

William Bradford was born in the north of England in 1590, while Queen Elizabeth I was still on the throne. Early in his life he was drawn to a group of Christians who wanted to go further than most of their contemporaries in reforming the English state church. They opposed practices like tax support for ministers and regulation of religious life by England's political authorities—which were common practices throughout Europe at the time. So serious was their opposition that they broke completely from the Anglican church. These "separatists," as they became known, first tried to work out their religious faith in England. But when pressure from the authorities became too great, they left in 1608 for Holland, at that time the most tolerant European nation. Soon discontent set in even there, for the separatists were afraid their children would lose the principles of their faith as well as the English language.

The next move was to seek refuge in America. For such a nondescript group of ordinary men and women this was audacious indeed. But it was an ironic "refuge" they found when the tiny band of fewer than 100 settlers arrived off the coast of Cape Cod at the start of winter in November 1620. In England, Bradford had been an ordinary member of the company. But when disease decimated the settlers, they turned to him for leadership because of his resolute stability and deep faith. From 1621 until his death in 1657, Bradford was continually reelected as governor of the Plymouth Colony. Between 1630 and 1651, he wrote a personal memoir for his own meditation and as a witness to further generations. This *History of Plimouth Plantation* was not published until 1856, but once published,

William Bradford was the leader of the Pilgrims who arrived at Plymouth Bay in 1620. The Pilgrims had to undergo much hardship before they got to the New World, and also after they arrived.

it became a landmark of American history. Bradford's vision of a world ruled by God's loving (if also sometimes mysterious) care would inspire many others. So too would his sense that God had a special plan for the Protestants who had come to the New World. Few, however, could write with the simple eloquence that Bradford used in describing the separatists' departure from Holland for the New World. "So they left the goodly and pleasant city which had been their resting place near twelve years; but they knew they were pilgrims and looked not much on those things but lifted their eyes to the heavens, their dearest county, and quieted their spirits."

Later Americans have both praised and criticized colonists in early New England for their efforts to keep life focused on God. What no one questions is that this very seriousness about God inspired some of the most capable individuals in American history. One person so inspired was Jonathan Edwards, who was born in 1703 and died in 1758 after living most of his life in Massachusetts. Edwards was an intellectually precocious youth who loved walking in the woods, in order to study natural phenomena (such as spiders spinning their webs). He also delighted in reading the Bible and studying Christian theology. During his pastorate of a Congregational Church in Northampton, Massachusetts, from 1729 to 1750, he was best known for promoting revivals of religion. In 1734–35 and again in 1739–41, he presided over periods when nearly everyone in Northampton, and many in the surrounding region, confessed their sins to God and sought diligently to practice religion as Edwards's sermons said it should be practiced. In these times of revival an unusual number of people found a sense of peace and security through faith in God. Edwards's written works tried to separate the husk of mere religious enthusiasm from the wheat of genuine Christian spirituality.

A Prayer of Jonathan Edwards

The following is the last part of the prayer offered by Jonathan Edwards at the conclusion of the funeral of David Brainerd in 1747. Brainerd was a missionary to Native Americans and was engaged to be married to one of Edwards's daughters. Brainerd's diary, which Edwards edited for publication, was filled with intense language of personal revival.

Oh, that the things that were seen and heard in this extraordinary person, his holiness, heavenliness, labor, and self-denial in life, his so remarkable devoting himself and his all, in heart and practice, to the glory of God, and the wonderful frame of mind manifested, in so steadfast a manner, under the expectation of death, and the pains and agonies that brought it on, may excite in us all, both ministers and people, a due sense of the greatness of the work we have to do in the world, the excellency and amiableness of thorough religion in experience and practice, and the blessedness of the end of such whose death finishes such a life, and the infinite value of their eternal reward, when absent from the body and present with the Lord; and effectually stir us up to endeavors that in the way of such an holy life we may at last come to so blessed an end. Amen.

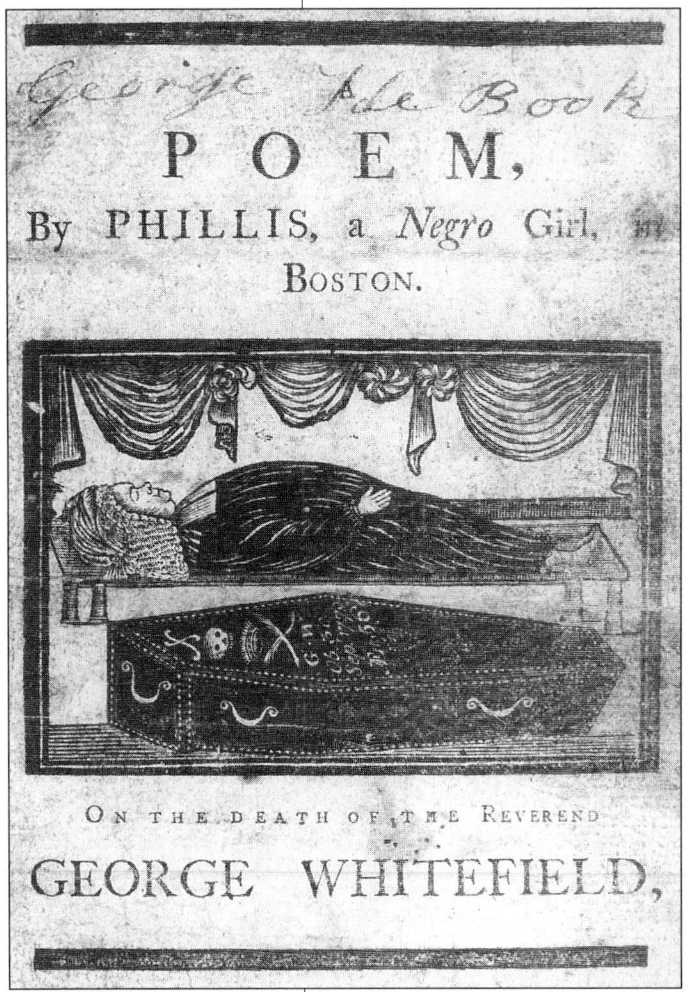
POEM,
By PHILLIS, a *Negro* Girl, in
BOSTON.

ON THE DEATH OF THE REVEREND
GEORGE WHITEFIELD,

Phillis Wheatley's poetic gift helped gain her freedom in 1773. Her poem on the revivalist George Whitefield showed that some African Americans had begun to accept Protestant Christianity for themselves.

As respected as Edwards became, however, it did not stop his own congregation from chafing under his ways. After a lengthy dispute, mostly over who would define the practices of week-to-week religious life, in 1750 Edwards was forced out of his Northampton church. That dismissal turned out to be a boon for students of theology, however, since Edwards spent the last years of his life writing a series of profound books that summarized themes he had been developing in private notebooks since his youth. When this latter writing was published—some not until the 20th century—it became obvious that Edwards was also a philosopher and theologian of exquisite intelligence. Only a few American Protestants after Edwards have been as honored as he was for their analysis of revivals or their abilities in theology. Nonetheless, Edwards was representative because of his keen interest in revival (which has been a perennial concern for Protestants in America) and also because he wanted to show how questions about God related to other spheres of life (another constant preoccupation for American Protestants).

An early American Protestant who lacked almost all of the social advantages enjoyed by distinguished clergymen such as Jonathan Edwards was Phillis Wheatley. Wheatley was born as a slave around 1753. In 1761 she was purchased by a new owner in Massachusetts, where she soon developed two interests. She was an eager participant at religious services, including some where the preacher was the Englishman George Whitefield. And she developed an unusual gift for poetry. When Whitefield, worn out by constant travel, died at nearby Newburyport in 1770, Wheatley responded with "An Elegiac Poem on the Death of the Celebrated Divine . . . George Whitefield," almost certainly the first poem ever published by an African American. The poem went out of its way to memorialize Whitefield's effort to include slaves and ex-slaves in his message:

> The greatest gift that ev'n a God can give,
> He freely offer'd to the num'rous throng,
> That on his lips with list'ning pleasure hung. . . .
> "Take him, ye Africans, he longs for you,
> Impartial Saviour is his title due;
> Washed in the fountain of redeeming blood,
> You shall be sons and kings, and Priests to God."

Wheatley's later life was difficult. Although she was given her freedom in 1773 and then made a trip to London, where her poetic gifts dazzled the English, she was subsequently deserted by her husband and left to die in poverty in 1784.

The experience of Phillis Wheatley, although unusual in some respects, was typical in the personal hope and consolation she found in a Protestant form of the Christian message. The recurring reality of such hope and consolation is one of the reasons why Protestants have enjoyed such a long and influential history in America.

A hint as to where that history began, before Protestants arrived in America, is found in the name of the great contemporary preacher, Martin Luther King, Jr. For the King family, which included several prominent Baptist ministers, to carry the name "Luther" was to wear a constant reminder of how and why Protestantism itself began.

MARTINVS LVTHERVS SS. THEOLOGIÆ D.

Redivivus. H e.

ANTITYPVS ORTHODOXAE RELI-

gionis Christiano-Lutheranæ & Idolamaniæ Pontificiæ, Anno Seculari Lutherano primo sacer.

Eigentliche Abbildung vnd Entgegensetzung der wahren Christlichen Lutherischen Religion/ vnd der Papistischen Abgötterey/ Gestellet auff das erste Lutherische Jubel Jahr/

MATH. XXV.

LEBEN. **TODT.**

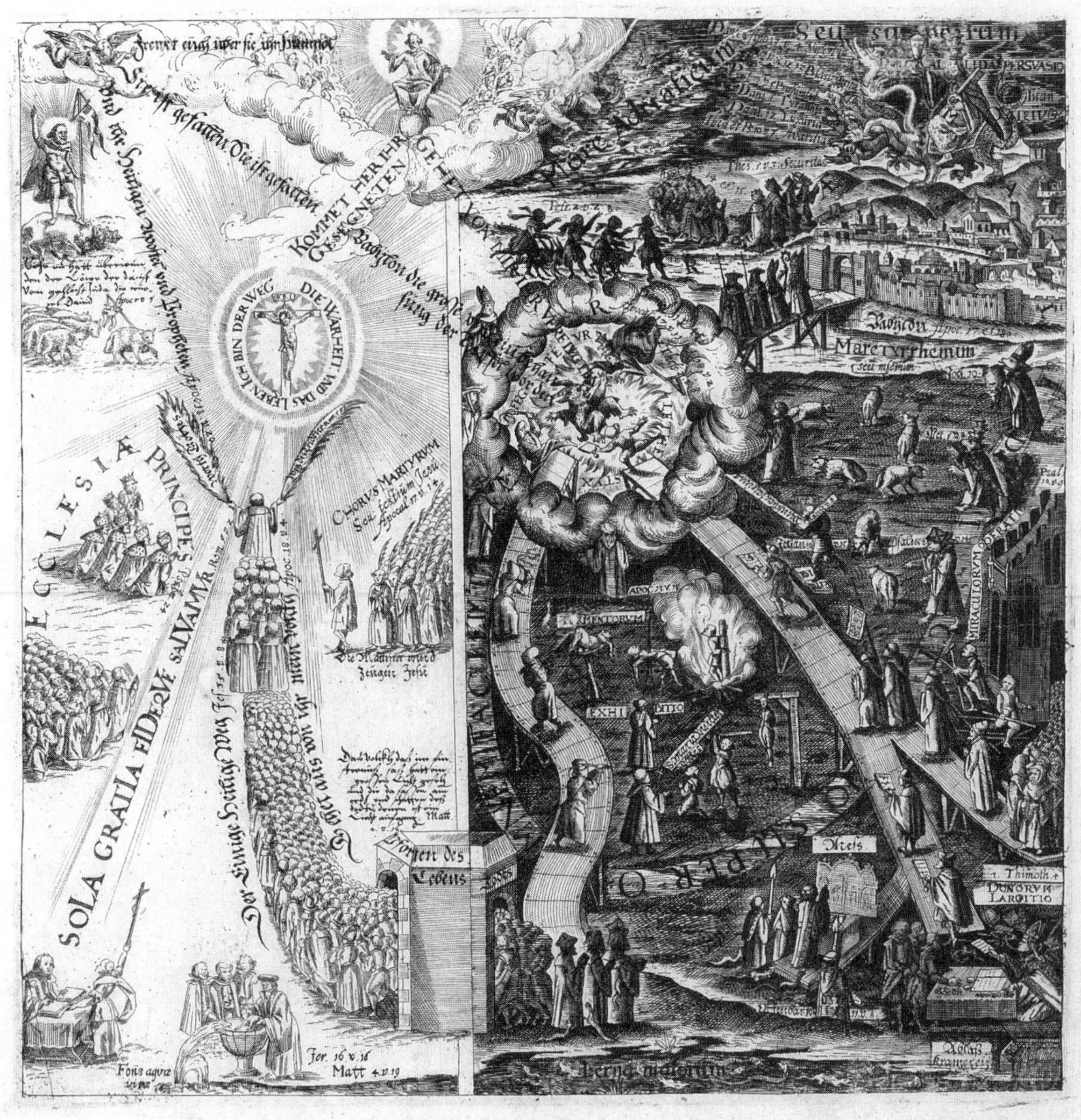

Chapter 2

Where Do Protestants Come From?

A terrified Catholic monk was the first Protestant. Martin Luther, a German Roman Catholic, was born in 1483 in Saxony, Germany. In 1505 he disappointed his father, who wanted him to be a lawyer, by entering a monastery. As a young monk, Luther did everything he was told to do: he prayed faithfully and he pursued the studies in Scripture and theology his supervisors requested. So conscientious was Luther in confessing his sins that fellow monks called him Dr. Scrupulant (for "scrupulous"). One of his superiors, exasperated by Luther's painstaking efforts to recite all his sins of attitude, urged him to commit some truly horrible crime so that he would not waste the confessor's time.

Some of the religious strife in early America simply continued what had gone on in Europe. This Lutheran print was published in 1617 to commemorate the centennial of the Protestant Reformation. On the left it depicts Christ, angels, God the father, heaven, and Martin Luther (far lower left); on the right side are hell, Satan, and the Catholic pope (triple hat, right center).

None of these labors worked. Luther was looking for the forgiveness of his sins from a gracious God, but all he experienced was terror at the perfections of God and despair about his own ability to do good. Part of the problem may have been Luther's, for he possessed an extraordinarily sensitive conscience. More of the problem, however, was in the Roman Catholic church of his day. The Catholic church had been Europe's prime source of religious direction for more than 1,000 years. As late as the 13th century, it had flourished under the vigorous leadership of dedicated reformers like St. Francis of Assisi and pious intellectuals like St. Thomas Aquinas. But over the course of the following centuries it had sunk into a long decline. It had been decimated by the Black Death of the 14th century. Throughout the 15th century quarreling over power between councils of bishops and various popes weakened it still further. Then at the end of the 15th century a series of worldly popes came to power who paid little attention to spiritual questions, precisely at the time when suffering souls like Martin Luther were begging the church to provide religious answers to religious problems.

Luther's spiritual struggle illustrated the nature of Protestantism. It was not a new religion, but rather an effort to correct problems in the very old religion of Roman Catholicism. As a reforming movement, the interpretation of ideas (often called "doctrines") became supremely important. That is why attention to what Luther thought is so vital for understanding later Protestant history.

Luther's great battle was his effort to understand the Bible. In his reading of the Bible, Luther was profoundly troubled by a pair of simple phrases from the Apostle Paul's Letter to the Romans (chapter one, verses 16 and 17): in "the gospel of Christ" is revealed "the righteousness of God." Luther later said that he hated the God he thought this passage described. On the one hand, it seemed to offer "the gospel" (or "good news" of peace with God and the forgiveness of sins). On the other hand, it promoted "the righteousness of God," which Luther took to mean God's high standards of perfection. What tore Luther apart was the suspicion that God was offering a false hope, since this alleged "good news" was nothing but a vision of divine perfection. All that vision did for Luther was to underscore how much of a sinner he was.

Luther found a way out by taking more seriously another phrase from the same passage: "the just [or righteous] will live by faith." The breakthrough was to see faith in Jesus Christ from a new angle. Luther knew all about the church's account of Jesus as God's Son who had come into the world to live a perfect life, die on the cross, and then be raised from the dead. Luther's life as a monk, and also as a priest, was organized around celebrating this divine-human life. The key, however, was to shift from regarding Christ as merely a messenger of God (and his perfections) to seeing him as the one who met God's standard of perfect righteousness on behalf of guilty sinners. With this insight Luther came to feel that the death of Christ on the cross made it possible for God to look upon sinners as if they were as perfect as Christ himself. Yet trouble arose as soon as Luther began to write and preach publicly about his new understanding of "the gospel."

A 19th-century depiction of Martin Luther tacking his 95 theses to the church door in Wittenberg, Germany, in 1517. This act sparked the widespread controversy that led to the Protestant Reformation.

In October 1517, Luther prepared a series of 95 theses, or propositions for academic debate, to criticize a traveling salesman who was hawking the indulgence papers Pope Leo X had authorized to raise funds for constructing St. Peter's Church in Rome. (An indulgence was a certificate that the church provided to lessen the penalties of Purgatory. More and more in Luther's day they were being sold to raise money for church, or even secular, projects.) It was a great surprise to Luther when his criticism was taken up with enthusiasm elsewhere in Germany, and then throughout much of the rest of Europe. Almost overnight, the struggles of a single monk became a first-order European crisis.

The hierarchy of the Catholic church reacted as if it were under siege and simply ordered Luther to shut up. But he was not a person who took such advice quietly. Increasingly, he stressed his understanding of the Bible's message as a justification for speaking out.

In April 1521, Luther was called before the Holy Roman Emperor, Charles V, to recant what he had written in criticism of the church. He refused. Luther's statement before Charles V was, in effect, the beginning of Protestantism: "Unless I am convinced by the testimony of the Scriptures or by clear reason (for I do not trust either in the pope or in councils alone, since it is well known that they have often erred and contradicted

Clergymen and bankers' agents in Europe selling indulgences to absolve purchasers of their sins. The banner symbolizes authorization from the pope.

themselves), I am bound by the Scriptures I have quoted and my conscience is captive to the Word of God. I cannot and I will not retract anything, since it is neither safe nor right to go against conscience."

The response throughout Europe to Luther's challenge was extraordinary. Luther became the leader of a "Reformation," because he was soon joined by many others who felt it was necessary to reform what was corrupt or stagnant in the church.

The term "Protestant" itself was coined in 1529 at another meeting called by Charles V. At this meeting, in Speyer, a number of princes and city councilmen who followed Luther and other reformers issued a "protestation" against what they regarded as corrupt church practices. The standard these "Protestants" followed was the Bible, or, as they put it, "the Word of God."

A long period of controversy followed the beginning of the Reformation. During the 16th century, Protestant voices were raised all throughout Europe. But a vigorous Catholic Reformation (also called the Counter-Reformation) largely checked the Protestant advance in southern and eastern Europe. Where Protestantism became established—England, Scotland, the Netherlands, Scandinavia, the northern German states, and a few of the Swiss cantons—it would continue as the dominant religion for the next several centuries. Significantly, these were the regions from which most of the first settlers came to North America.

Protestants developed an almost infinite variety of denominations, churches, and movements. But almost all Protestants have continued to stress in one way or another at least some aspects of the principles that defined Protestantism in the 16th century:

By grace alone. Early Protestants, such as Luther, insisted that human salvation was a gift from God accomplished by Christ's saving death and resurrection, commonly referred to as "justification by faith alone."

Scriptura sola (the Bible alone). Protestants affirmed that the Bible should be the preeminent guide for religious life. Some Protestants in the 16th century spoke as if they affirmed the Bible without acknowledging any other religious authorities at all. But most Protestants, then and now, have usually viewed the Bible as the supreme religious authority over all other authorities.

The church as the believing people of God. The earliest Protestants retained the Catholic practice of organizing churches territorially. That is, if you lived in a region, you were part of that region's church. Increasingly, however, Protestant views of redemption moved them toward defining the church as the group of individuals who were called out of the world by the message of Christ in the gospel. Right from the first, Protestant stress on the Word (or words) of God made the sermon the key activity of church life. This newer view of the church provided a heady sense of liberation from the rituals of the past. But it also led eventually to a tremendous diversity of individual Protestant congregations and denominations.

The priesthood of all believers. Protestants upheld the privileges of all professed Christians to come before God in Christ without human intermediaries. In Luther's terms, each believer was to be a "little Christ" to his or her neighbors. Ministers and professional theologians differed from other Christians in their functions, but not in their spiritual status.

The sanctity of all callings. Protestants rejected medieval distinctions between secular and sacred callings. Again in Luther's words, "The works of monk and priest in God's sight are in no way whatever superior to a farmer laboring in the field, or a woman looking after her home."

By 1600, Protestants were divided into several family groups. Some of the division was due simply to geography, as the interests of a region coalesced around a local leader. Some was due to the influence of powerful rulers. Some division, however, was due to the inability of Protestants to agree among themselves. Protestants united to emphasize the authority of the Bible over the Roman Catholic pope. But it proved far more difficult to agree positively on just what the Scriptures said about shaping new churches.

Of the various Protestant families, the "Reformed" would be most widely represented in early America. Reformed Protestants were sometimes also called "Calvinists" because of the great reputation of John Calvin, the 16th-century reformer of Geneva, Switzerland. Reformed Protestants put even greater stress on the authority of the Bible than many other Protestants. They shared a belief in predestination, or the call of God, as the most important element in turning people from themselves to Christ. And they believed resolutely that every action in daily life should be done to honor God. The Reformed were strongest in Switzerland, southern Germany, Holland, and in some regions of Britain. The churches in America that grew from these beginnings are the Congregationalists, the Presbyterians, and the Reformed (Dutch and German).

Two other kinds of Protestants from the European continent were also early immigrants to America. A few Lutherans from Sweden came to what is now Delaware in the 1630s, but the significant Lutheran presence in America had to wait until immigration from Germany in the 18th century. Large-scale German and Scandinavian settlement in the United States during the 19th century also added to the Lutheran presence. Not surprisingly, these Lutherans tended to maintain Luther's distinctive teachings. For example, unlike almost all other Protestants, Lutherans held that the two Protestant sacraments of communion and baptism communicated a real (not just symbolic) presence of Christ to those who took part.

The other European brand of the Reformation to make an early appearance in America was the "Anabaptists," which means "those who are baptized again." Anabaptists were the radicals of the Reformation.

They tried to organize their lives by observing strictly what Jesus said and did. Most radically, Anabaptists rejected the centuries-old practice of baptizing infants. Instead, they held that only adults should be baptized and only when they had personally announced their desire to follow Jesus. In this desire to follow Jesus literally, Anabaptists also rejected participation in warfare. They took their pacifism from words of Jesus in the New Testament such as Matthew 5:39, "whosoever shall smite thee on thy right cheek, turn to him the other also." Because in Europe, the baptism of infants made children into citizens as well as church members, opponents of the Anabaptists thought their beliefs were seditious. They held that Anabaptists were promoting the dissolution of society, and so some Protestants joined with Catholic authorities in persecuting Anabaptists mercilessly. The most successful body of Anabaptists were the

Lutherans on their way to America (center) pass through the German city of Leipzig in 1732. By 1740 there were 95 Lutheran churches (mostly German) in the 13 colonies that would become the United States.

Mennonites, who were formed by the efforts of a former Catholic priest from the Netherlands, Menno Simons (1496–1561). The first American Mennonites migrated to Pennsylvania in 1683. Other smaller groups of Anabaptists—the Amish (a European spinoff from the Mennonites) and the Hutterian Brethren—came later.

Reliable statistics on Protestants are difficult to acquire because of the diversity and fragmentation of the movement itself. Yet modern estimates offer an indication of where Protestants have spread since the 16th century. As of the late 1990s, about 450 million people could be counted as active adherents of Protestant churches around the world. About one-fourth of that number lived in North America. For the last several decades, while the proportion of residents in the United States identifying with Protestant churches has remained steady, Protestant expansion has exceeded population growth in some Asian countries like Korea, some urban regions of Central and South America (especially Brazil), and in many areas of Africa.

In the United States, about 8.5 million Lutherans, almost 5 million Presbyterians and Reformed, and approximately 500,000 Mennonites, Amish, and other Anabaptists trace their religious ancestry back to the European Protestantism of the 16th century (although the Presbyterians are rooted also in Scotland, England, and Ireland). The other American Protestants are affiliated with churches that came into existence after the 16th century but which usually have a historic connection of some kind to Protestantism in its earliest days. The Protestant movements that originally meant the most in America came from the British Isles. Since European colonization in what would become the United States began primarily from Britain, it was only natural that religious developments there exerted a great influence in what took place on this side of the Atlantic.

The Reformation in England had two distinct aspects: religious and political. Making up the religious movement were reform-minded students, ministers, and laypeople who read Luther's works eagerly as soon as they became available. The religious beginnings of English church reform eventually broadened to include a number of remarkable figures.

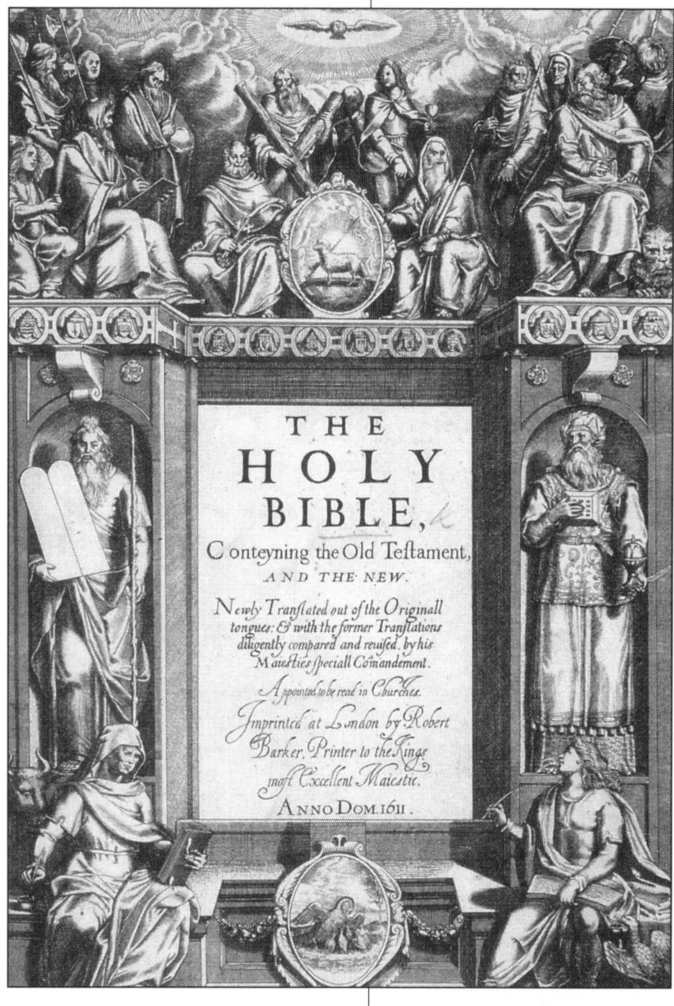

The King James Version of the Bible from 1611 was the primary translation of the Scriptures for most American Protestants until well after World War II. This elaborately illustrated title page is from a 1612 printing.

A wandering scholar and preacher, William Tyndale, was so inspired by Luther's biblical explanation of justification by faith that he resolved to provide England with an up-to-date translation of Scripture. Tyndale's heroic labors on that project were hampered by many difficulties and then ended when he was executed for religious and political reasons. But the substantial portion of the Bible he translated inspired others to take up the task, and his work greatly influenced the King James (or Authorized) Bible of 1611 and continues to influence English translations of the Bible to this day.

A sometimes wishy-washy public servant, Thomas Cranmer, was the English reformer who exerted the longest-lasting impact after Tyndale and his Bible. In 1533 Cranmer was appointed the Archbishop of Canterbury, England's chief religious figure, mostly because he had figured out a way to let King Henry VIII divorce his first wife, Catherine of Aragon (mother of a daughter, Mary, but no sons). Cranmer worked behind the scenes to move England in a Protestant direction. Especially influential was a summary of Christian teaching he prepared (later known as the Thirty-Nine Articles) and a collection of religious services for daily and Sunday use known as the *Book of Common Prayer*. These literary works have remained the backbone of the Church of England (also known as the Anglican Church), as they have been also for Anglican churches around the world. In the United States the Episcopalians are descendants of Thomas Cranmer's Anglicanism.

Thomas Cranmer was the Archbishop of Canterbury who helped his monarch, Henry VIII, move England from Roman Catholicism to the Protestant Church of England. His *Book of Common Prayer* is the ancestor of prayer books still used in the American Episcopal Church.

The other aspect of the English Reformation was at first very different from the push for religious reform. It concerned the personal and political intentions of Henry VIII (who ruled 1509–47) and his three children who succeeded to the English throne: Edward VI (ruled, 1547–53), Mary Tudor (1553–58), and Elizabeth I (1558–1603). In the late 1520s Henry VIII broke with the pope, who had refused Henry's desire to divorce Catharine and marry Anne Boleyn (who became the mother of Elizabeth). Henry then set up an autonomous Church of England. But he remained a believer in traditional Catholic teaching even as he was busy plundering church and monastic lands for his own purposes.

Edward VI, the sickly son of Henry and his third wife, Jane Seymour, was a sincere Protestant who encouraged considerable Protestant activity during his brief rule. But when he died prematurely and was succeeded by his half-sister Mary, an earnest Roman Catholic, Protestantism was once again in difficulty. Mary tried to return England to the Catholic church, but failed.

Under the crafty Queen Elizabeth, Protestants finally won. Although Elizabeth was conservative in religion as well as politics, she made a version of Protestantism into the official state church. In this church she hoped to find a unified, stable religion that could provide security for the English nation. Elizabeth also inspired England to fight against the leading Catholic nations of Europe, especially Spain.

Despite these advances, some English Protestants were not satisfied with Elizabeth's actions. They felt she was too willing to undercut true religion in order to protect her own security. The ones who were most dissatisfied became known as "Puritans," as they were first called derisively, because they wanted to "purify" the church of "popish" remnants such as kneeling for communion, observing holy days, and providing special garments for ministers. In fact, many Puritans wanted to exclude from

England's religion everything that was not commanded directly by the Scriptures. Not surprisingly, strife followed.

From the Puritan movement came several spinoffs that played a major role in America. William Bradford, the early governor of the Plymouth Colony in Massachusetts, was a member of one small, peace-loving, but also rigorous group. Another offshoot from the Puritan movement was led by the former Anglican minister John Smyth and his lay associate Thomas Helwys at the turn of the 16th century. Smyth, Helwys, and their associates became convinced that Elizabeth's regulation of the church as well as the historic Christian practice of baptizing infants were both hopelessly corrupt. They too led their followers at first to Holland. More important for later American history, they began the Anabaptist practice of baptizing adult Christians on the basis of their own personal professions of faith. Thus were born the Baptist churches whose descendants became so numerous in America.

The religious tumults of the 16th century spilled over also into Scotland and Ireland. In Scotland, John Knox inspired a reform of that northern kingdom, which was at the time still independent from England. Knox, a fiery preacher, attacked the papacy and the Catholic Mass while he assiduously promoted the diligent Calvinism and the lay education for which Scotland would become renowned. The Catholic queen of Scotland, Mary Stuart, opposed Knox, but she was no match for the ardor of his religious vision.

Ireland was also affected by the efforts of Henry VIII and Elizabeth to spread their influence. In 1537, Henry decreed an end to Ireland's subjection to the papacy, although most of the Irish paid no attention. Elizabeth repeated her father's decree, set up an Anglican state church in Dublin, and also exported English and Scottish Protestants to settle in the North of Ireland. From Scotland and Ireland would come thousands of settlers, many of them Reformed Protestants, to the New World.

The earliest Protestants who came to America from Europe were predominantly from the British Isles rather than the Continent. And so the Protestantism of early American settlers reflected more the straightforward earnestness of British Reformed religion than the doctrinal complexities

The Pilgrim's Progress

A book written by a tinker from Bedford, England, who never set foot in America, became a much beloved work for generations of American Protestants. John Bunyan enjoyed little formal education, but he mastered the Bible and became a writer of genius. Because he was an Independent (or Congregationalist) who refused to obey laws supporting the Anglican state church, he spent much time in jail. His Pilgrim's Progress *(1684) is a full-length allegory of faith and hope. It traces the long, perilous journey of a pilgrim, "Christian," from the City of Destruction to the Celestial City. In this passage the pilgrim loses the great burden that he has carried for a very long time.*

He ran thus till he came at a place somewhat ascending; and upon that place stood a *Cross,* and a little below in the bottom, a Sepulcher. So I saw in my Dream, that just as *Christian* came up with the *Cross,* his burden loosed from off his Shoulders, and fell from off his back; and began to tumble; and so continued to do, till it came to the mouth of the Sepulcher, where it fell in, and I saw it no more.

Then was *Christian* glad and lightsom, and said with a merry heart, *He hath given me rest, by his sorrow; and life, by his death.* Then he stood still a while, to look and wonder; for it was very surprizing to him, that the sight of the Cross should thus ease him of his burden. He looked therefore, and looked again, even till the springs that were in his head sent the waters down his cheeks. Now as he stood looking and weeping, behold three shining ones came to him, and saluted him, with *Peace be to thee:* so the first said to him, *Thy sins be forgiven.* The second stript him of his Rags, and cloathed him with change of Raiment. The third also set a mark in his forehead, and gave him a Roll with a Seal upon it, which he bid him look on as he ran, and that he should give it in at the Celestial Gate: so they went their way. Then *Christian* gave three leaps for joy, and went on singing.

The fiery Calvinist preaching of John Knox helped establish the Presbyterian church in Scotland. In this picture Knox is shown appealing directly to Scotland's Catholic queen, Mary Stuart.

of Martin Luther, or the pacifism of the Anabaptists. They resembled earnest Catholic Christians of the Middle Ages by practicing asceticism, or the disciplined organization of all life and attitudes for the glory of God. But unlike the monks and nuns of the Middle Ages, these Reformed Protestants practiced their discipline for God *in* the world. Family life, business practices, political decisions, management of leisure time—all such concerns were pursued with religious seriousness.

The early Protestants who came to America were seeking not a private space to be religious but an open space to transform with their religion. Later contributions by Protestants to American democracy, capitalism, individualism, patterns of settlement, and voluntary associations all sprang—sometimes for good, sometimes for ill—from the character of the 16th-century Reformation.

The QUAKERS SYNOD.
G: Whitehead
Call over yᵉ List, Are none of Truths enemies here
are the doors shut
W. Penn.
W: Bringly
yea the doors are lockt
deputies
B: Bealing scribe
deputies
deputies
church canons
yᵉ Journal of G. Fox
deputies
deputies
deputies
deputies
deputies
deputies

Chapter 3

Protestants in Colonial America, 1607–1789

In early 1756, the Presbyterian preacher Samuel Davies, who had been working as a missionary pastor in Virginia for nine years, received a new shipment of hymnbooks. What meant most to Davies about these hymnals was how eagerly they were put to use by African-American slaves. Although Davies was not a social radical, and even owned one or two slaves himself, he was unusual for his day in spending a great deal of time preaching to blacks, giving them books, teaching them to read, and urging them to take part in the services of his church. He wrote back to England about a special kind of singing that occurred with the new hymnbooks: "Sundry of them ['the *poor Slaves*'] have lodged all night in my kitchen; and, sometimes, when I have awaked about two or three o-clock in the morning, a torrent of sacred harmony poured into my chamber, and carried my mind away to Heaven. In this seraphic exercise, some of them spend almost the whole night."

This incident illustrates several important features of Protestant life in colonial America. Christian evangelization of African Americans had begun. The new form of Protestant piety that Davies promoted, known as evangelicalism, was spreading fast. But tension was also growing between a European form of religion, where state churches monopolized religious practice in a single region, and an American form, where diverse forms of faith co-existed in the same place.

In a Quaker meeting there were no regular preachers. Instead, all worshippers, including women, were invited to speak when moved by the "Inner Light of Christ."

Davies' experience shows that Protestants in the American colonies were meeting their first challenge—which was to survive. It also shows how they were responding to a second great challenge—which was to adjust. The nature of that second challenge is illustrated by the actions of Davies, a Presbyterian minister descended from Welsh parents and preaching to African-American believers in a colony controlled by English-descended Anglicans who owned slaves to work their plantations.

In Europe almost all the Protestant churches (except the Anabaptists and a few Baptists) had been supported by the state. They were *established* by law; each church enjoyed a religious monopoly in its own region. In each of the American colonies, however, members were present from several Christian traditions almost from the start. In addition, social contact among blacks from several places in Africa, several kinds of Native Americans, and several varieties of Europeans created a rainbow of ethnic diversity unlike anything experienced in the Old World.

The first English colonists to secure a permanent foothold in North America came in 1607 to Virginia. Early Virginia included a number of earnest Protestants associated with the Church of England (thus, Anglicans). John Rolfe, for example, in 1614 married Pocahontas, daughter of the Algonquian ruler Powhatan, not only to promote peace with the Indians but also to share the Christian faith: "I will never cease," he wrote of his desire to have Pocahontas become a Christian, "untill I have accomplished, & brought to perfection so holy a worke, in which I will daily pray God to blesse me, to mine, and her eternall happiness." By comparison with the Puritan colonies of Massachusetts and Connecticut, though, Anglicans in Virginia were disorganized, half-hearted, and ineffective. The early entrance of slavery into Virginia greatly complicated religious, as well as legal and commercial relationships, among settlers. The far-flung character of Virginia's settlement—with farms and estates isolated by Virginia's many rivers as well as by the large amounts of land required for growing tobacco—also made it difficult to establish effective churches.

Difficulties also abounded for settlers in New England. But in the colonies that eventually became the states of Massachusetts and Connecticut a different kind of Protestant forged a different kind of society.

In 1630, or 10 years after the small body of Separatists arrived at Plymouth, a much larger group of Puritans arrived at Boston with the intent of making the Massachusetts Bay Colony into a society that honored God. Their numbers would reach 40,000 by the end of that decade. Their motives grew out of the accumulated frustrations of the previous generation. What Puritans had not been able to accomplish in the Old Country—that is, to reform the churches and sanctify society—they were determined to do in the New.

Later judgments on the Puritans often get the story wrong. They did not come to American in search of freedom as such, nor were they the Calvinist tyrants pictured by some historians. Rather, the Puritans sought liberty to establish a society that followed the law of God as they understood it. Dissenters from the Puritan way in New England would be treated almost as harshly as Puritans had been handled by king and bishop in England. But for those in New England who could accept the larger purposes of the Puritan leaders, possibilities existed for political stability, social harmony, and religious fulfillment available nowhere else in the world during the 17th century.

The leader who showed the Puritan movement at its best was John Winthrop. Elected the first governor of the Massachusetts colony before the settlers left England, Winthrop was re-elected to that same post for most of his life. As a young man he had experienced a classic Puritan conversion in which grave concern about his own unworthiness and fear of God's holiness gave way to solid trust in Christ and steady determination to do the will of God. In 1630, on board the ship *Arbella* as it was crossing the Atlantic, Winthrop preached a noteworthy sermon. He talked about the Massachusetts settlement as "a citty upon a hill" which the world would watch to see if the Puritans lived up to their high calling as God's servants. Winthrop's greatest concern in the sermon, however, was not to speculate on the distant future but to urge his fellow colonists to make Massachusetts "a model of Christian charity."

Once in New England, Winthrop proved to be an extraordinarily capable leader. He had to experience the death of family members, occasional electoral setbacks, and considerable anxiety over political

The Voice of Anne Bradstreet

Anne Bradstreet migrated with her husband, Simon, to Massachusetts with the first wave of Puritans in 1630. The Bradstreets moved among the political elite of Massachusetts, but physical weakness brought on by a childhood bout with rheumatic fever meant that Anne risked death in giving birth to each of their eight children. Anne Bradstreet became the first notable poet in the English-speaking American colonies. Many of her poems, such as the stanzas that follow (slightly modernized) from "Verses upon the Burning of Our House, July 10th, 1666," are subtle expressions of her religious faith. After the poem memorializes the goods and memories destroyed in the fire, the last stanzas turn to broader considerations:

Then straight I began my heart to chide:
And did thy wealth on earth abide?
Didst fix thy hope on mouldering dust
The arm of flesh didst make thy trust?
Raise up thy thoughts above the sky,
That dunghill mists away may fly.

Thou hast an house on high erect;
Framed by that mighty Architect,
With glory richly furnished,
Stands permanent though this be fled.
It's purchaséd, and paid for, too,
By Him who hath enough to do—

A price so vast as is unknown,
Yet, by His gift, is made thine own.
There's wealth enough; I need no more.
Farewell, my pelf [worldly goods]; farewell, my store;
The world no longer let me love.
My hope and treasure lie above.

Governor John Winthrop was the leading citizen of early Puritan Massachusetts. He was sometimes demanding with his fellow Puritans, but never asked them for more than he would do himself.

upheavals in the mother country. Most notably, he and his colleagues created out of virtually thin air a workable, equitable government for Massachusetts. Yet through all these experiences he did not lose his personal equanimity, a magnanimous attitude toward friends and many of his foes, and steady faith in the goodness of God.

The Puritan settlement that actually took shape in Massachusetts, as well as the sister colony of Connecticut, never reached the Christian perfection Winthrop sought. In both colonies the godly regularly quarreled about exactly how best to interpret the Scriptures. Soon Winthrop, like William Bradford in Plymouth, began to fear that Massachusetts was showing more concern for material prosperity than for Christian fellowship.

Despite failure to live up to their founders' loftiest goals, the Puritan settlements achieved remarkable results. In the Puritan churches, several generations of diligent ministers poured great energies into the two (or sometimes even three) weekly sermons that were the center of community life. In both Massachusetts and Connecticut, the sermons functioned as a source of political direction and news from afar, as well as religious instruction. Most of them stressed a Puritan variation of the central

Reformation themes: human unworthiness before God, the mercy of Christ in redemption, and the satisfaction in living a life of gratitude toward God.

The other kind of sermon preached by the ministers was for special occasions, for instance, the annual election of the legislature, for militia exercises and going off to war, to mourn in times of drought, or to celebrate a bountiful harvest. On these days the Puritans ministers talked more about what the people should be doing in response to God's dealings with their land.

There were many Puritan ministers who made a special mark. John Cotton of Boston was known as a "searching" preacher because of how carefully he applied biblical passages to ordinary life. Thomas Shepard had gone through lengthy spiritual traumas as a young man, which may be one reason why he was so effective as a minister in Cambridge, where the Puritans' fledgling college began in 1636. That school was named for John Harvard, a minister who died young and gave his library to promote education among the Puritans. The forcefulness of preacher Thomas Hooker's personality made Boston too small for both him and John Cotton, so Hooker moved to Connecticut, where he helped establish the town of Hartford and through his books became one of New England's most influential intellectual leaders. But no Puritan minster exceeded the energy or painstaking religious diligence of Increase Mather and his son Cotton, who championed the values of the early settlements far into the next century.

John Winthrop and other leaders of the early Puritan colonies were not democrats in any modern sense of the term. In fact, they could persecute those who held what they considered the wrong religion. For example, between 1659 and 1661 the Massachusetts Puritan authorities hanged four Quakers, members of a more radical Protestant group than themselves, when the latter insisted upon returning to Boston after they had been banished.

Winthrop, however, also believed that the fellowship of Christians was important and that the church should be at the heart of a properly functioning society. These convictions led Massachusetts to promote more democracy than England had ever experienced. As originally conceived, the Massachusetts Bay Company was to be governed through leaders chosen by "freemen" at annual elections. The "freemen" were the investors who had put up the money to start the colony. But once they were in Massachusetts, Winthrop and other officers arbitrarily changed the definition of "freemen" to mean any adult male who was a member in good standing of a local church. In this way, Winthrop broadened political responsibility to the godly in general, but also connected the exercise of that political responsibility with the goals of the churches. The later development of democracy in America eventually eliminated a formal place for religion, but that later democracy grew from seeds planted with a definite religious purpose.

Puritan churches in New England came to be called "Congregationalist" because individual congregations chose their own ministers and controlled many aspects of their religious lives. These Congregationalists kept alive early Puritan concerns for several generations. Only in the 18th century, with widespread economic and intellectual change, quarrels among the churches, and a political revolution in public life did Puritanism fade away. Even so, Puritan traits of earnestness, orientation to tasks, and moral seriousness remained to shape much of later American history.

Success in pursuing the Puritan way of Congregational churches did not, however, take place without opposition. Two significant dissenters in early New England history showed how Puritanism could create its own most serious critics.

Roger Williams was much too thorough a Puritan to get along in a colony run by other Puritans. Williams came to Massachusetts in 1631 with a reputation for personal gentleness, but also for rock-hard stubbornness in his convictions. Almost immediately he ran into trouble because he could not keep those convictions to himself. He quickly expressed the opinion, for example, that the Puritan rulers had no right to the American Indian lands. He also let it be known that he thought it was a fundamental religious error for magistrates to enforce attendance at church since true Christianity had to proceed without coercion from any external authority.

As an old man in 1680, Roger William wrote a letter of protest to the town of Providence, Rhode Island. As he had so many times before, Williams defended the principle of personal freedom under God.

Roger Williams entred his Protest agnst ye Illegalitie or Lawfullnes of this aforesaid meeting as not being Lawfully Called in our Kings Majesties name by his officer a Magistrate at three dayes warning: & Consequently he protested agnst all Acts & Orders & Adjournments yt were or should be made, upon yt illegal factious, & dangerous foundation:

Roger Williams.

This protest is entred on ye 48th page of ye Town booke of ye Entry of Town orders:

₱ Dan: Abbott Towne Cl:

These views were dangerous in Massachusetts, a community where leaders like John Winthrop were trying to establish a complete system of tightly interwoven religious and civic responsibility. Expelled from the colony in 1636, Williams went to the head of Narragansett Bay and founded the city of Providence in what would soon be the colony of Rhode Island. In a long, trouble-strewn career as Rhode Island's dominant figure, Williams tried to treat Native Americans with the kind of respect they rarely received from Europeans. He also opened his colony as a place of "soul liberty" to others who wore out their welcome with the Puritans. But some of these other exiles proved unwilling to tolerate even the benevolent democracy of Rhode Island and so caused Williams no end of grief. When England's Civil War began in the 1640s he returned to the mother country and published a book that pleaded his case for greater toleration. This remarkable tract, *The Bloody Tenent of Persecution for Cause of Conscience in a Conference between Truth and Peace,* had almost no impact when it came out in 1644. But it later became important to religious groups such as the Baptists, who joined Williams in rejecting governmental control of religion, and then to lovers of democracy of all sort.

Another memorable figure whose dissent shook the Puritan colonies was Anne Hutchinson. Hutchinson migrated to Massachusetts with her family in order to remain under the teaching of their English pastor, John Cotton. The difficulty she posed was her seriousness about acting on Cotton's principle that God's grace *freed* people in Christ. Hutchinson gathered first women, and then a mixed group of women and men, into her home to discuss Cotton's sermons and to probe other religious questions. The authorities were particularly distressed at her idea that since believers possessed the Holy Spirit within, they did not need a public law to restrain their behavior without.

Winthrop and the Massachusetts authorities put Hutchinson on trial in 1638 for "antinomianism" ("living as if there was no law") or the teaching that a believer did not become holy by obeying the law. Hutchinson more than held her own in court, mostly by skillfully quoting from the Bible and citing the views of Cotton concerning the freedom of believers in Christ. But at the end Hutchinson overreached herself. When she had all but silenced her accusers, she let slip the claim that the Holy Spirit communicated with her directly, not just through the Scriptures. In the language of the Reformation, this was proof that she was an "enthusiast," someone who falsely claimed divine inspiration and so undercut the authority of the Bible. The response was swift. Hutchinson and her followers were banished.

A few years later, Massachusetts authorities nodded their heads in pious self-satisfaction when they heard that the whole Hutchinson clan was wiped out in an Indian attack. Later commentators were not so sure. In Anne Hutchinson they saw a legitimate Puritan emphasis both liberating the use of Scripture and empowering laity, especially laywomen, to figure out religious meanings for themselves. Many have concluded that this story led as naturally to the liberties Anne Hutchinson sought as to the regimented society John Winthrop constructed.

In the 18th century the Protestant potential for stable responsibility as well as for disruptive creativity were even more obvious than during the previous century. Because both the times and the religious picture were changing fast, the story for Protestants and their churches became much more complicated. As an indication of these changes, the population of the American colonies jumped from about 250,000 in 1700 to nearly 1.2 million in 1750, a number that then doubled once more in the next 25 years. Economic life also expanded dramatically, and there was nearly continuous political excitement.

The most notable public event before the American Revolution was persistent warfare with France. That warfare was important for religion because it confirmed the Protestant colonists' in their belief that the Roman Catholic religion of France was the foe of freedom, and that the pope was probably the Antichrist out to destroy everything the Protestants held dear.

During America's tumultuous 18th century there was rapid growth in the number of Protestant churches and a major change in the emphases of religion. The Congregational churches of New England and Anglican churches in Virginia, Maryland, and other southern colonies continued to be the officially established churches. But more and more other Protestants were taking advantage of the openness of the New World to found their churches as well.

Even before the end of the 17th century, the Society of Friends (or Quakers) were a powerful presence in Pennsylvania. The Quakers had been one of the radical sects that flourished in England during the 17th century. They matured under leaders such as George Fox and soon developed a forceful Christian pacifism. One of the Quakers' most important converts was William Penn, son of a British admiral. In 1681 Penn acquired a huge tract of land in the New World and in 1682 laid out the

city of Philadelphia, partly as a commercial venture, but even more to provide his fellow Quakers and other religious minorities a safe haven.

In this 18th-century engraving from a painting by Benjamin West, William Penn signs a peace treaty with the Indians in 1681. Penn made his colony a welcoming place for his fellow Quakers, but also for Christians from many other denominations.

By the time the Quakers were moving to Pennsylvania and the nearby colonies that were later amalgamated as New Jersey, a number of Dutch Reformed churches were already established in New York, which had been a colony of Holland until it was taken over by the English in 1664. By the end of the 17th century, a few Mennonites and Lutherans had arrived in Pennsylvania, mostly from Germany. Quite a few churches were also being set up in the middle colonies by Calvinist Protestants from Germany—members of the German Reformed churches. The first wave of settlers from Scotland or from Scotland by way of Ireland (the Scots-Irish) were setting up Presbyterian churches in Pennsylvania, New Jersey, and on Long Island. And several different kinds of Baptist churches were being gathered in New England, New York, and points farther South.

Not long after the turn of the 18th century, the variety of Protestants increased even more. Moravians and humble farmers called simply

The Moravians, German pietists who had been persecuted in Europe, came to the New World early in the 18th century and pioneered missionary activity among Native Americans. Moravian brethren and sisters are depicted here in prostrate worship.

Brethren came from Germany to the New World (mostly Pennsylvania) with the message of Pietism. Pietism was the renewal movement in European churches that stressed an interior religion of the heart and self-sacrificing Christian service more than formal allegiance to the institutions and creeds of the churches. By the middle of the century, even more expressions of Protestantism—such as the Shakers, who followed Mother Ann Lee, and the Universalists, who felt God would ultimately redeem all humanity—had appeared in the American colonies.

In 1769 the first preachers commissioned by John Wesley for service in America arrived in the New World. Wesley's movement for reform and renewal within the Church of England had already been given the name "Methodist," since it emphasized a systematic approach to Christian piety and self-sacrificing social service. Although Methodism spread quite slowly in America until after the Revolution, the arrival of those first itinerant (or traveling) preachers was extremely significant. After the Revolution the Methodist church became the fastest-growing form of Protestantism in

America, and Methodist standards of piety, worship, and service exerted a huge impact on American religious life.

A statistical account suggests the tide of Protestant diversity that was rolling into the American colonies. In 1700, Congregationalists and Anglicans constituted almost two-thirds of all churches in the 13 colonies; by 1780 the proportion of Congregational and Anglican churches was reduced to approximately one-third, even though their actual number had increased. In colonial America almost all the churches were Protestant. At the time of the American Revolution, there were only about 50 Roman Catholic churches in the 13 colonies, and only a few scattered Jewish settlements, mainly in New York, Rhode Island, and Philadelphia. Representatives of other religions were still virtually unknown.

St. John's Episcopal Church is a National Historic Landmark and the oldest surviving place of worship in Richmond, Virginia. It was in this church that Patrick Henry delivered his famous speech, "Give me liberty or give me death."

Formal education in the colonies was also strongly influenced by Protestants, with all the major colonial colleges more or less under the influence of regional Protestant bodies. Thus, Congregational influence was dominant at Harvard and Yale in New England, Presbyterian influence at the College of New Jersey (later Princeton University), Anglican influence at the College of William and Mary in Virginia, and a variety of informal Protestant influences at the institutions that later merged into the University of Pennsylvania in Philadelphia.

Although almost all colonial churches were Protestant, the great variety of Protestant churches created a new and unsettling problem. The European pattern of one church in one place had been set up by Congregationalists in New England and by Anglicans in Virginia and elsewhere in the South.

But by the mid-18th century, this European pattern was breaking down fast. Not only were Baptists, Presbyterians, Methodists, and others seeking their own space in Congregationalist Massachusetts and Anglican Virginia, but in the middle colonies of New York, New Jersey, and Pennsylvania, so many different Protestant groups had taken root that it was a practical impossibility to favor any one of them over the others.

In this situation a major change occurred in the character of Protestantism. That change was partly a response to religious diversity in the colonies. But it also came from American participation in the 18th century's major shift in religion itself. The new element is usually identified by the name "pietism" on the Continent and by "evangelicalism" for Britain and North America. The essence of pietism or evangelicalism was a movement away from formal, outward, and official religion to personal, inward, and heartfelt religion.

The most visible symbol of the new evangelicalism in America was the traveling Anglican preacher George Whitefield. Whitefield had been an Oxford undergraduate of very modest means when he was recruited into a "Holy Club" in which John Wesley and his hymnwriter brother Charles were prominent.

In a radical departure from traditional practice, Whitefield preached wherever the people could be gathered, which was usually outside of the churches, at any hour of the day or night, and sometimes in immense crowds. For another, he wore his Anglican ordination lightly and eagerly cooperated with Protestants of every sort who would back his work—including Baptists, Presbyterians, Congregationalists, Moravians, the early Methodists, and more. Whitefield prepared his sermons carefully, but in a sharp break with standard practice he delivered them extemporaneously, talking directly to—not at—the people. In yet another innovation, Whitefield and his associates were eager and expert exploiters of newspapers and pamphlets.

Whitefield's message featured conversion, or the "New Birth," a phrase taken from Jesus' dialogue with the Jewish leader Nicodemus as recorded in the third chapter of the Gospel of John. Whitefield was a riveting preacher with great rhetorical skills. When he thundered forth the stern demands of God's law, when he wept at the pitiful state of lost sinners, when his faced turned radiant in describing the glories of union with Christ, people listened. They listened in England, Wales, Scotland, and Ireland, and they listened throughout the American colonies during the seven different trips he made there over a 30-year period.

George Whitefield used fliers, advertisements, and especially newspapers to spread word of his meetings. He was the most popular speaker of any kind in 18th-century America.

During his second visit to the colonies, in 1740, Whitefield preached extensively at his home base in Savannah, Georgia, but also in Charleston, South Carolina, Philadelphia, New York, Boston, and many smaller sites. His tour of New England that fall was one of the most dramatic events in American religious history. For more than a month Whitefield preached almost every day to crowds of up to 8,000 spellbound listeners, and at a time when the total population of Boston was not much more than that.

One of those who came to hear Whitefield during his famous New England tour of 1740 was a farmer, Nathan Cole, who lived near Middletown, Connecticut. Cole's diary records the sensation: "When I saw Mr Whitfield come upon the Scaffold [that had been erected for the sermon] he Lookt almost angelical; a young, Slim, slender, youth before some thousands of people with a bold undaunted Countenance . . . . And my hearing him preach, gave me a heart wound; By Gods blessing: my old Foundation was broken up, and I saw that my righteousness would not save me."

Whitefield was the central figure in a diffuse movement called the Great Awakening. This movement was not a tightly organized affair, but rather a series of memorable preaching occasions that sparked a major turn toward a more personal, emotional, inward, and experiential religion.

In simplest terms, that shift marked the passing of Puritanism and the rise of evangelicalism as the dominant Protestant expression in America. In fact, as a result of groups inspired by Whitefield's kind of preaching and sometimes encouraged by the careful theological writing of Jonathan Edwards, New England's traditionally unified churches fragmented. But outside New England, the revival fires associated with the Great Awakening did more to build churches than to fragment them. These new churches were founded without worrying about establishment—Baptists in the middle colonies and the South, Presbyterians in Virginia, German immigrant congregations in Pennsylvania, and soon Methodists everywhere.

Because this new form of religion stressed individual exertion in conversion and the religious life, it was much more attuned to the expanding, market-oriented societies of the 18th century than to the ideals of stable church establishments. Whitefield took his dynamic message to the people. He masterfully exploited the interest of the press in controversy.

In the wake of George Whitefield and the broader colonial Awakening, many changes were immediately evident. Religious bodies that stressed freedom from state control (such as the Baptists) or that relied on their own initiative rather than state connections (such as the Methodists) flourished. New hymns, with fresh melodies and direct, affecting lyrics, rejuvenated group worship. Soon Samuel Davies and other Americans were writing new hymns. The best of these composers was William Billings of Boston, who published *The New England Psalm-Singer* in 1770. It was the first book of totally American music published on American soil. Soon other Protestants were also writing their own music. The most notable of such groups were the Moravians. These German pietists founded towns like Salem, North Carolina, and Bethlehem and Nazareth, Pennsylvania, where the churches featured choirs, organs, trumpets, violins, outdoor performances at Christmas and Easter, and a great deal of sophisticated Baroque music.

The revivalism promoted by Whitefield was also a religion that could be transported easily to the frontier. It required only an earnest preacher and an audience of people who were concerned about their souls before God. The older established churches struggled when they tried to expand to the frontier. But the revivalists, who abandoned state-church religion and formal educational requirements for ministers, got the job done.

The older pattern of religion conceived as unity for a whole community did not pass away immediately. Connecticut and Massachusetts retained vestiges of their colonial establishments far into the next century.

The frontispiece of William Billings' *New England Psalm Singer,* published in 1770. It set a high standard for the huge number of Protestant hymn books that followed.

In addition, the most active Protestants among the nation's founders all tried at first to devise some scheme for having governments support the churches. John Witherspoon, the Presbyterian president of Princeton, was the only clergyman to sign the Declaration of Independence. He proposed a plan for government to support more than one religion in a single region, a plan that was similar to one advocated in Virginia by the faithful Anglican and patriotic orator Patrick Henry. But these plans did not succeed. Religious leaders shaped by the colonial revivals joined founders such as Thomas Jefferson and James Madison in working toward the First Amendment to the U.S. Constitution, which prohibited the federal government from establishing any one particular religion even as it guaranteed to all citizens protection for the free exercise of religion.

In the 18th century Protestants also carried their message beyond the main bodies of British colonies. African Americans, for example, were present from the start of colonization, but Protestant leaders paid scant attention to them until much later. Slavery, which became well established

The Duty of CIVIL RULERS, to be nurſing Fathers to the Church of CHRIST.

A

SERMON

PREACHED BEFORE THE

GENERAL ASSEMBLY,

OF THE COLONY OF

CONNECTICUT,

At HARTFORD;

ON THE DAY OF THE

ANNIVERSARY ELECTION;

MAY IXth, 1765.

By EDWARD DORR, A.M.

Paſtor of the firſt Church in HARTFORD.

HARTFORD;

Printed by THOMAS GREEN, at the HEART and CROWN, oppoſite the STATE-HOUSE.

Several American colonies sponsored annual "election sermons," in which a minister was asked to address the legislature. The United States' new constitution of 1787 broke from that tradition by prohibiting the national government from supporting any one particular religion.

in the southern colonies, and which also existed or was promoted in the middle and northern colonies, was put in place without a great deal of conscious reflection.

Religious neglect of African Americans began to change during the Great Awakening. Whitefield, though himself a slave owner, went out of his way to preach to African Americans and also encouraged black converts to take an active part in colonial churches. Samuel Davies in Virginia was only one of several other proponents of the new evangelicalism who tried to bring African Americans into their churches. In the years after the Awakening, several of Jonathan Edwards's students used religious arguments to attack the slave system. They held that it was a violation of the "being" of humans of any sort to be held in complete bondage by others.

Major breakthroughs for the spread of Protestant Christianity among African Americans did not, however, occur until the era of the American Revolution. The formation of black churches was beset with every kind of social prejudice and legal disadvantage, but emerge they did. The first continuing black church was the Silver Bluff Church in Aiken County, South Carolina, where an African-American preacher, David George, established a congregation around 1773 or 1774. As for many other slaves, the American Revolution was a godsend to George. American patriots were trying to throw off the "slavery" of Britain's Parliament, but for those in bondage, like George, the British were the agents of liberty. When the British abandoned Savannah, George went with them to Nova Scotia, where he helped establish the first black Baptist churches in what would later become Canada. Several other African-American churches were founded in and around Savannah during

The First African Baptist Church of Savannah, Georgia, was originally called the Ethiopian Church of Jesus Christ. It was founded by Andrew Bryan, a slave and an ordained minister, and his wife Hannah around 1788.

and after the Revolution. The significance of such preliminary moves to start African-American churches was profound. From the religion of the slaveholders, slaves were catching a message of liberation. For those whom everyone in the colonies considered the dregs of society, the chance to practice Christian faith was conveying a message of hope, dignity, and purpose.

The Revolutionary War was the last religious, as well as political, episode in America's colonial history. Considerable religious debate occurred over the war. Loyalty to Britain, which was often rooted in religious convictions, led to the migration of significant numbers of colonists to Canada or back to Britain. Many Anabaptists, Quakers, and pietists rejected entirely the violence of the war. But most Protestants decided in favor of the patriots' cause, and some preachers were among the most vociferous supporters of American independence.

And so the churches adjusted also to independence, as growing numbers of Protestants had continually adjusted during the colonial era. In the face of serious challenges, Protestants were making the transition from Europe to America. Life in a new nation and a new century would bring them unprecedented opportunities, but also unanticipated perils.

THE WAY OF GOOD & EVIL.
ETERNAL LIFE
THE WORD
DESTRUCTION
EVERLASTING PUNISHMENT
GALLOWS
MURDER
ADULTERY
ROBBERY
FORGERY
SWEARING
CHEATING
STATES PRISON
RUM
DUELLING. HYPOCRISY
INTEMPERANCE
GAMBLING
GAMEING
FALSE
LYING
IGNORANCE
FIGHTING
HOUSE OF SIN
PRIDE
DEATH
VANITY
PROFANE
LUSTING
SHAME
DISEASE
SCHOOL HOUSE
HUMILITY
FAITH IN CHRIST
PURE OF HEART
RIGHTEOUSNESS
AVOIDING EVIL
THE COLLEGE
Every way of a man is right in his own eyes: but the LORD pondereth the heart.
THE HOUSE OF GOD
PEACE
INDUSTRY
HEALTH
DISOBEDIENCE TO PARENTS AND TEACHERS
OBEDIENCE TO PARENTS AND TEACHERS
TRUTH
WISDOM
THE WORLD

Chapter 4

Protestants in Charge, 1790–1865

In 1862, Harriet Beecher Stowe visited the White House. When Stowe, who was less than five feet, approached the six-and-a-half-foot-tall President Abraham Lincoln, he leaned over her and said wryly, "So you're the little woman who wrote the book that started this great war." Lincoln was referring to *Uncle Tom's Cabin,* which Stowe had published in 1852, and which was later republished in huge numbers and in many forms, including a widely performed play. On one level, the novel was an effective polemic against slavery. On another level its portrait of Uncle Tom, who suffers the lash of the evil overseer Simon Legree so that two other slaves can escape, was a Christ figure intended as spiritual encouragement against all kinds of human bondage. The extraordinary popularity of this work testified to the resonance between the Protestant values that drove Stowe's writing and the tastes of a wide American audience.

Those values also had been aggressively promoted by her father, Lyman Beecher, a leading Congregationalist minister who had deliberately chosen to move from New England to Cincinnati as a way of extending Protestant influence into the opening West. The positive side of Beecher's activity bore fruit in the creation of many voluntary organizations aimed at spreading Christianity and alleviating human suffering. The negative side was heightened belligerence against those whom Beecher considered enemies of Protestant civilization. For much of the antebellum period, this meant Roman Catholics.

Parlors in 19th-century American homes often were decorated with religious prints like this one. Its contrast between virtues and vices illustrated graphically the worldview of many ordinary Protestants.

No account of 19th-century American Protestantism is complete without the Beecher family. In this portrait, the patriarch (the Rev. Lyman Beecher of Connecticut, Boston, and Cincinnati) sits front row center, while on the far right are the author of *Uncle Tom's Cabin* (Harriet Beecher Stowe) and the nation's most popular preacher of the Civil War era (Henry Ward Beecher of the Plymouth Congregational Church in Brooklyn, New York).

White evangelical Protestants such as the Beechers, were, of course, never "in charge" of the United States in the same way that established Protestant churches had monopolized religion in European countries. Rather, the strength of Protestants in the two generations before the Civil War rested on a great rise in adherence to the churches as well as energetic attention to reform of society. It also rested on successful adaptation to a new political environment.

The U.S. Constitution was new in a very specific way for the churches. The First Amendment in the Constitution's Bill of Rights (1789) guaranteed unprecedented freedom of religion: "Congress shall make no laws respecting an establishment of religion, or prohibiting the free exercise thereof." This principle of religious freedom was radically new in its time. Many colonial Americans retained European attitudes, especially the expectation that the state would favor one church and that this established church would in turn support the state. Deeply troubled, traditionalists wondered how religion could survive if it was not protected by the state.

The American answer was that religious people could take care of themselves. And they did so remarkably well. As American churches began this experiment in freedom, Europeans maintained old patterns.

The result in the centuries after 1800 is that American religious bodies, including Protestants, have flourished in great (even chaotic) variety, while religious adherents in Europe have steadily declined. One very important reason for that difference is that in America, with its constitutional freedom of religion, ordinary people have taken charge of their own religious destinies. Churches have not, for the most part, suffered by their associations with social elites, since the churches have enjoyed the people's allegiance only so long as they could keep it.

The Methodists were the key to Protestant expansion in the early United States, and no Methodist made a greater contribution than Francis Asbury, an English follower of John Wesley who began his career as a traveling preacher at the age of 13. In 1771 Wesley asked for volunteers to go to America, and Asbury responded eagerly. Before he died, Asbury traveled nearly 300,000 miles, mostly on horseback, into all the former 13 colonies and the new states of Tennessee and Kentucky. Asbury himself followed the advice he later gave to younger Methodist preachers: "Go into every kitchen and shop; address all, aged and young, on the salvation of their souls." Asbury's relentless concern for souls also extended to the social welfare of humanity. He argued against slavery, he willed his modest estate to the Methodist publishing house, and he took a strong stand against hard liquor at a time of rampant drunkenness, especially on the frontier.

Francis Asbury kept tight reins on the Methodists' traveling preachers and so ensured a measure of discipline in the United States' most rapidly growing religious movement. Besides his constant activity as a preacher, Asbury also took a strong stand against slavery and urged abstinence from hard liquor.

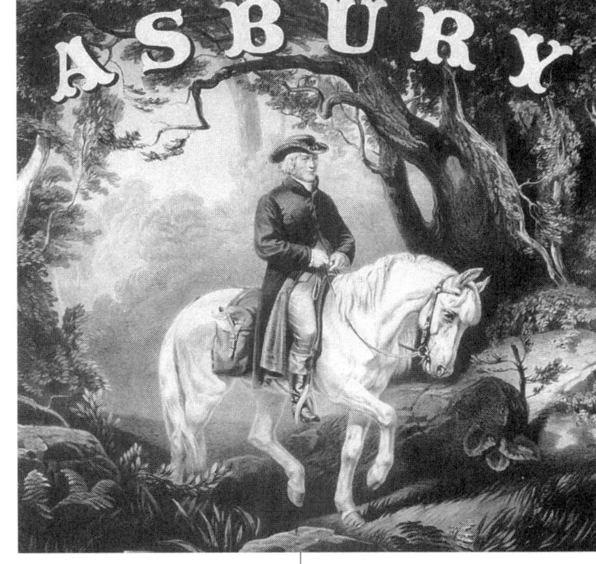

In December 1784 Asbury and his associates met in Baltimore to establish a formal Methodist organization in America. To an unusual degree Methodism combined the democratic style of the New World with a measure of control reminiscent of the Old. Methodist preachers aimed their message directly at the common people and were eager to set up small class meetings and local church services where laypeople were expected to do much of the work. Above all, the early Methodists were earnest. Asbury once described his schedule like this: "My present mode of conduct is . . . to read about one hundred pages a day; to preach in the open air every other day; and to lecture in prayer meeting every evening." Despite difficulties, he soldiered on: "The water froze as it ran from the horse's nostrils. . . . I have suffered a little by lodging in open houses this cold weather; but this is a very small thing when compared to what the dear Redeemer suffered for the salvation of precious souls." Asbury was joined in his work by hundreds, and then thousands, of eager coworkers. When he arrived in America there were four Methodist ministers looking after about 300 laypeople. By the time of his death in 1816, there were 2,000 ministers and more than 200,000 members of Methodist congregations. This rate of expansion continued after Asbury's death as well. The Methodists had about 30 churches (or preaching stations) in 1780. That number rose to 2,700 by 1820, and to an incredible 19,883 by the start of the Civil War in 1861. (In 1860 there were only slightly more United States post offices in the entire country than there were Methodist churches.)

The success of Methodists in organizing churches in cities and towns, on the frontier and in the countryside, in the settled East and the opening West, had a considerable impact on theology in America. The dominant theology of the colonial period had been Calvinistic, with a strong emphasis on God's control over the path that sinners took from the self to God. George Whitefield innovated in many things, but in his theology he held resolutely to Calvinism. For Whitefield, humans responded to God's initiatives, rather than originated the move to God in themselves.

The Methodists, by contrast, were Arminians, a name taken from Jacob Arminius, an early opponent of Calvinist teaching in the Netherlands. As Arminians, the Methodists shared many convictions with the Calvinists—belief in the holy Trinity, belief in the Bible as a revelation from God, and belief that God redeemed sinners by His grace. What was different in Arminianism was a stronger sense of human capability. Methodists believed that people had been given freedom by God to choose for or against the offer of salvation. With their founder John

Wesley they also held that faithful exercise of the will could move a person toward a position of Christian "perfection" (or an end to willful sin after conversion).

The rapid growth of the Methodists did not proceed without important changes taking place in the movement. During the age of Asbury, the norm for a Methodist minister was incessant travel, poverty, and a spartan life. Gradually over time, the intense focus on laypeople meeting together to read the Scriptures, confess their faults to each other, and encourage the group in godly living gave way to a religion organized around public services in a church building under the oversight of a "settled," formally trained minister. Methodists may have been paying a price as they became more like other denominations, but it was the price of success. Their expansion in the early republic was one of the most remarkable feats in all American history. More than any other single event, that expansion was responsible for the wide cultural influence that Protestants exerted in antebellum America.

However dynamic they were, the Methodists were only one aspect of a great Protestant mobilization that historians sometimes call "the Second Great Awakening." In every dimension, this mobilization relied heavily on the techniques of revivalism.

Revivalism took many forms. In the early years of the Second Great Awakening, for instance, scholarly college presidents in the East, such as Timothy Dwight at Yale, guided revivals among their students and then placed revived students as pastors of already established churches. Their emphasis was on an orderly, disciplined response to the Christian gospel. At about the same time on the Western frontier, revival was much more exuberant. At one of the most memorable meetings, which occurred at Cane Ridge, Kentucky, in August 1801, thousands of people congregated for a "camp meeting." This gathering featured preaching day and night from Presbyterian, Baptist, and Methodist ministers, and from exhorters both black and white. The results were electrifying. Many participants fell down as if struck dead, while others laughed out loud, barked like dogs, or experienced "the jerks." After the excitement wore off, longer-term

The combination of energetic participants and detached observers was characteristic of many camp meetings. The camp meeting was one of the most important ways by which Protestants brought their message to settlements on America's rapidly expanding frontiers.

results were the creation of many new churches, especially Methodist and Baptist churches.

The essence of revivalism was direct appeal by a dedicated (often passionate) preacher to individuals who gathered expressly for the purpose of hearing the revivalist's message. Most revivalists were men, although there were also some lively women preachers, such as Harriet Livermore, who in January 1827 became the first woman to preach in the U.S. Capitol. Her appearance shows that the separation of church and state applied most directly to institutions, not to what occurred voluntarily, even in public facilities.

The purpose of the revival meeting was always the same: to convert lost sinners to faith in Christ and, through the reformed behaviors of the saved, to improve society. Revivalism was thus a perfect religious fit with the social and political values of the new United States. Revivals were democratic in their appeal to all types and levels of society. They were egalitarian in preaching the same message to all. They fit the spirit of the American 19th century by appealing to individuals to change themselves. But they were also traditional in providing a picture of God similar to what many had heard in older churches.

For most of the middle and southern United States, the Protestants who knew how to put revivalism to fullest use were the Baptists. The Baptist message was a time-honored one of sinners needing to find God's grace. As the name implies, Baptists held that individuals should be baptized by full immersion in water after they had consciously professed faith in Christ. Baptist notions of responsibility stressed the freedom of local groups from outside influence. Baptists also developed many strong local leaders—often laypeople—who, with or without formal education, took the initiative in forming new churches. Baptists, thus, were uniquely situated to stress the liberating, individualistic aspects of both the Christian message and the politics of the new United States.

"Farmer-preachers" became the characteristic symbol of Baptist strength in the early United States. Such ministers were part of the citizenry during the week, but then assumed the role of preacher and pastor in the formal church services, while still remaining very much "of the people." John Leland, who preached in New England and Virginia, was one of the most notable early Baptists. While in Virginia he supported Thomas Jefferson and James Madison in their efforts to disestablish the Anglican church. Then he moved back to Massachusetts, where he fought the same battle against the state-supported Congregational

The depictions on this certificate were intended to serve as motivation for missionary service. The scenes of "heathen darkness" and "Christian civilization" both represented romanticized Protestant portraits.

church. The growth of the Baptists was only slightly less sensational than the growth of the Methodists. Where there were only about 460 Baptist churches in the country at the end of the American Revolution in 1780, that number rose to well over 12,000 by 1860.

Baptist leadership, although usually intensely local, did include several preachers and educators who gained national recognition, such as Francis Wayland, the longtime president of Brown University in Providence, Rhode Island. Wayland was an ardent advocate of missionary work and also authored several widely used textbooks on ethics, politics, and philosophy.

Energetic labors by leaders such as Asbury, Leland, and Wayland explain why the Methodists and Baptists expanded so rapidly in the early 19th century. The same kind of energy, with something of the same kind of results, led to the creation of several denominations freshly minted in the new American nation. Most important of these were the churches of the Restorationist movement, which sought, in effect, to begin Christianity over again by stripping away the accumulated baggage of the centuries. Its name comes from the effort to "restore" Christianity to the purity of the New Testament. Its leaders were Alexander Campbell, a Scottish immigrant, and Barton W. Stone, a plain-speaking Marylander who participated in the great migration to Kentucky of the 1790s. Campbell and Stone, feeling a disillusionment with traditional churches, broke away in the effort to restore the type of primitive Christianity they thought they could see in the New Testament's Book of Acts.

Campbell and Stone created separate movements called "Disciples of Christ" and "Christians only," respectively. The movements were alike in seeking to follow the New Testament literally, in practicing baptism by immersion for adult converts, and in stressing the autonomy of local congregations. In the early 1830s, the two churches joined together as the Christian Church (Disciples of Christ). Church statistics reveal again the strength of an appeal to antitraditional, lay-oriented, self-starting religion in the early days of the new American nation. By the time of the Civil War, there were just about as many Disciples churches (2,100), concentrated mostly in the upper South and the lower North, as the old colonial

Nineteenth-century America was a hotbed of new religious movements. Among the most enduring were the churches of the Restorationist movement, whose early leaders included (clockwise from top) Thomas Campbell, Barton W. Stone, Alexander Campbell, and Walter Scott.

churches, Episcopalian (2,150) and Congregationalist (2,240). (In their later development, the Restorationist churches would divide into groups known as the Churches of Christ, the Christian Church, and the Disciples of Christ, each of which retains considerable vigor in selected areas of the United States.)

The upsurge of Protestantism that began shortly after 1800 continued steadily into the middle decades of the century. More than any other person, Charles Grandison Finney exemplified the power of revivalism. Finney was born in Connecticut but exercised his most memorable religious work at the expanding margins of American society, first in upstate New York and then in Ohio. He was trained as a lawyer, but in 1821 experienced a dramatic conversion that immediately redirected his energies to preaching. Finney began as a revivalist in small towns such as Evans Mills, Antwerp, and Perch Rive, New York. Soon he graduated to small cities, including Troy, Utica, and Rochester. Finally, he took his message to the great cities of the Eastern seacoast: Boston, New York, and Philadelphia. In 1835 Finney moved to Oberlin College in Ohio, which became his headquarters for the rest of his life.

Finney was a wholehearted advocate of "new measures," many of them taken over from the Methodists. He encouraged women to speak publicly at his meetings; he urged people who were sorry for their sins and who wanted to be converted to gather at an "anxious bench" and pray for salvation; and he often held "protracted meetings" that lasted for weeks or even months at a time. These innovations were bitterly opposed by leaders of the older churches. Some of Finney's opponents also worried about the great stress he placed on the ability of individuals to turn to God as an exercise of their own willpower without divine assistance. Surely, they thought, this was carrying self-reliance too far. He was also criticized for urging converts to become active social reformers against drunkenness, slavery, luxurious eating, mistreatment of the mentally ill., and the Masonic movement. Finney's charisma as a speaker—his clear penetrating gaze, vigorous speaking voice, and relentlessly logical style—made him every bit as influential as the era's great politicians.

If Charles Finney represents the vigor of Protestant revival, Phoebe Worrall Palmer illustrates the strength of its inner spiritual renewal. Phoebe Worrall was raised in New York City, where she married a wealthy physician, Walter Palmer. During her early adulthood, Mrs. Palmer, as a faithful Methodist, earnestly pursued John Wesley's outline for a perfect Christian life. From 1835 she conducted a "Tuesday Meeting for the Promotion of Holiness" in the New York home of her sister, Sarah Worrall Lankford. At that gathering she encouraged guests to talk of their experience with God and she outlined her own idea of "entire sanctification," or perfect consecration to God. Especially after a memorable religious experience on July 26, 1837, when Palmer reported a special manifestation of the Holy Spirit, she became a dynamic proponent of what would come to be known as "holiness" or, in other circles, "the higher Christian life."

Palmer observed many of the conventions of the 19th century about public activity for women. But this diffidence was not a restraint. She contributed many essays to periodicals, she instructed many people of high estate and low in her understanding of godliness, and she participated in more than 300 revival meetings in the United States, Canada, and Britain. Several of her books sold hundreds of thousands of copies. *The Promise of the Father* (1859) forthrightly defended women's right to preach on the basis of biblical passages such as Joel 2:28 ("your sons and daughters will prophesy"). She was also one of the leaders in urban reform movements, such as a project to bring housing, education, work, and regular religious services to the Five Points district, one of New York City's worst slums. Palmer's emphasis upon the Holy Spirit as a source of spiritual illumination and power also anticipated the spread of Holiness denominations, including the Church of the Nazarene, which occurred toward the end of the 19th century. It also helped to pave the way for the Pentecostal movement of the 20th century.

Phoebe Palmer's skill at publicizing a vision of Christian "holiness" made her one of the most influential religious figures of her day. She was equally adept as a platform speaker and as a publisher of books and magazines.

The specifically religious efforts of figures such as Finney and Palmer would not have influenced American society so directly if religion had remained neatly separated from the wider world. In fact, however, Protestants enjoyed a powerful vehicle to link private faith and public life. That vehicle was the voluntary society, which proved ideal for taking advantage of the Constitutional separation of church and state.

Voluntary societies were organizations set up independently of the churches and governed by self-sustaining boards for the purpose of addressing a specific problem. Their genius was that they provided a way for individuals from different denominations to pool their concerns, energies, and money while also enjoying great flexibility in meeting the rapidly developing social changes in an expanding U.S. society.

Congregationalists from New England took the lead (often moving out to New York or the "West" of the Ohio River Valley), but they were soon joined by many Presbyterians, representatives of the German and Dutch Reformed Churches, and some Episcopalians, Methodists, Quakers, and Baptists. The first large voluntary societies had distinctly religious purposes, such as the American Board for Foreign Missions (1810) and the American Bible Society (1816). But soon broader social purposes were also being served. Whether providing books and Bibles by traveling vendors, organizing to improve the treatment of the insane, attacking the institution of slavery, or reaching out to outcasts such as prostitutes, the Protestant voluntary agencies took in hand the social conversion of the United States.

As they did so, they opened up unusual opportunities for women. The sisters Sarah and Angelina Grimké, for example, were born in South Carolina to a family of slave-holding Episcopalians. But when they moved to Philadelphia and the sisters joined the Quakers, they began to speak out against slavery and other social ills. Angelina Grimké's tract arguing for the end of slavery, *An Appeal to the Christian Women of the South* (1836), won her immediate recognition in the new abolitionist movement, but also gained her the reputation, in both the North and South, as a dangerous radical. Later both sisters became public speakers for the American Anti-Slavery Society. When such speaking in public by women was attacked, Sarah responded with a biblically-based defense in her *Letters on the Equality of the Sexes, and the Condition of Women* (1838). The avenue provided the Grimké sisters by voluntary associations was an avenue opened up for many who had earlier performed religious duties only in private.

It is important to realize, however, that not all Protestants participated in the coordinated activities of what has been called "the Protestant United Front." A longstanding resentment of "Yankee meddling" encouraged hostility to the voluntary societies. Since Northern, usually urban and often Congregationalist or Presbyterian, spokespeople were the leaders of the voluntary agencies, they were often received with suspicion by Baptists and Disciples (in both North and South) who worried about the loss of local autonomy. Many others, especially in the South, felt that Northern arguments about slavery represented an unwarranted, uninformed intrusion.

At the heart of this dispute lay contrasting Protestant attitudes toward the republican foundations of American government. Almost all Protestants in the early United States accepted the guidelines of the founding fathers for the relationship of religion and society. The federal government would not sponsor any particular denomination and it would also try to ensure the broadest possible space for the exercise of religion. In turn, the churches were expected to give up overt political action. But both the nation's founders and major Protestant leaders looked to the churches to strengthen the moral character required for a republican government. Writers and speakers on all sides appealed to the slippery term "virtue" to make this argument. Sometimes "virtue" was defined as a self-sacrificing attitude toward public service, sometimes as private holiness before God. In either case, almost all Americans thought that "virtue" in the citizenry was required to preserve liberty, to check the natural tendency of governments to expand their power, and to make the checks and balances of the Constitution actually work for the well-being of society. The great difference of opinion between those who eagerly embraced the national plans of the (mostly Northern) voluntary societies and those (often Southern) people who resented their activities concerned the fate of virtue under the influence of these societies. Their defenders regarded national organization as a rational, efficient way to encourage citizens to pursue personal and public virtue. Their opponents saw the same agencies as bloated monsters threatening the liberty and virtue of people in their local settings.

Angelina (top) and Sarah Grimké were born into a Southern slave-holding family. But after they moved north, they became leaders of the abolitionist movement and also argued for expanded rights for women.

A second group of Protestants also felt excluded from the national activities of the great voluntary societies, but for a different reason. These were the members of immigrant Protestant churches that still maintained

THE

PAPAL CONSPIRACY

EXPOSED,

AND

PROTESTANTISM DEFENDED,

IN THE LIGHT OF

REASON, HISTORY, AND SCRIPTURE.

BY

REV. EDWARD BEECHER, D.D.

BOSTON:
PUBLISHED BY STEARNS & CO.,
91 WASHINGTON STREET.
1855.

Edward Beecher, a younger member of the Beecher clan, carried on the anti-Catholic polemics of his father Lyman. When this pamphlet was published in 1855, a major political movement (the American Party) was making opposition to the immigration of Catholics a central plank in its platform.

the languages or practices of the homeland. Lutherans from Germany or Scandinavia, pietist groups such as the Church of the Brethren, Anabaptists such as the Mennonites, or Reformed congregations from the Netherlands sometimes resented efforts by national voluntary societies as so much meddling with their own treasured traditions.

The great surge of Protestant expansion after the American Revolution affected the country in many ways. The clearest sign of that impact was the widespread suspicion of the Roman Catholic church that Lyman Beecher did so much to fuel. Protestant opposition to Catholicism was most explosive in the Eastern cities that by the 1830s were home to increasing numbers of Catholics. In 1834 a Boston mob burned the

Ursuline Convent in nearby Charlestown because of stories (unfounded) that young girls were being held there against their will. The prewar climax of anti-Catholicism was the formation of a political movement, the American Party. Its members were called "Know Nothings" because they refused to divulge information about their organization. Know Nothings felt that immigrants, especially Roman Catholics, were damaging America's Anglo-Saxon stock and subverting American liberties by maintaining loyalties to a despotic foreign power—that is, the pope. In 1854 the American Party elected 75 members to the U.S. House of Representatives, but its influence quickly declined in the rapid political changes that led to the Civil War.

The nearly universal influence of the Bible on American speech is another illustration of Protestant expansion. Throughout this period the Scriptures as translated in the King James Bible were the one indispensable book in the country. Publication of the King James Bible during the colonial period was reserved to designated British printers. But not long after the Revolutionary War for Independence, American publishers

The American Bible Society, which was founded in 1816, has remained one of the most successful voluntary societies in the United States. From its founding to 1980 it distributed more than 3 billion copies of the Bible, the New Testament, or portions of Scripture. During the Civil War, Scriptures were provided to soldiers on both sides of the struggle.

began the incredible industry of Bible publication that survives with great force to this day. Between 1777 and 1865, at least 1800 different editions of English-language Bibles were published, the overwhelming majority of them the King James Version. By 1830, the American Bible Society was distributing over 300,000 copies of the Bible (in whole or parts) each year.

Protestants today can find much to celebrate, and non-Protestants much to admire, in the period of American history when Protestants exerted such an influence on the institutions and values of the United States. But the flourishing of Protestantism in the early United States also contained sharp ironies that led to tragedy as well as to triumph. Even as Protestant Christianity was conquering a country, it found that it could not conquer itself, at least that part of itself that had become entwined with the system of black chattel slavery. The ironies of Protestant success in prewar America were also visible in relationships with other minorities like the Cherokee Indians.

A peace treaty in 1794 stimulated a cultural revival among the Cherokees of northern Georgia, eastern Tennessee, and western North Carolina. It also opened the way for white missionaries to begin their work. While the Cherokees built roads, organized themselves politically, rendered their language in writing, and began to print their own books and newspapers, they also welcomed the missionaries. A slow but steady acceptance of the Christian faith followed, and also an eagerness to accept American political institutions.

During the administration of President Andrew Jackson, however, the evangelism of the missionaries and the Americanization of the Cherokees both received a fatal blow. After the discovery of gold in northern Georgia about the time of Jackson's election in 1828, the lust of white settlers for Cherokee land increased. The result was a forced removal of the Cherokees from Georgia to the West. The missionaries who had come to the Native Americans as bearers of American civilization as well as of Christianity, confronted a terrible dilemma. They now were forced to watch their country, supposedly the embodiment of Christian civilization, turn violently against a people that had accepted their message.

Many of the missionaries caved in to the pressure and agreed to the removal. But others protested vigorously, even to the point of civil disobedience. Evan Jones and his son John B. Jones, two Northern Baptists, stood up for Cherokee rights and then journeyed with the outcasts to Oklahoma, where they continued the work of evangelization and education. The ministers they trained formed the backbone of a sturdy network of Cherokee Baptist churches that eventually developed in the new tribal lands. But missionary support for the Cherokee was not enough. The United States, bearing the gifts of Christian faith and democratic politics, destroyed a tribal people that was working hard to accept those gifts.

The tragedy of slavery was even greater. Protestantism had very much to do with strengthening the moral purpose of all major groups caught up in the dilemma. Most importantly, the early decades of the new United States witnessed a dramatic rise in African-American churches. The same period also saw strong Protestant support for abolition. But it also witnessed a great strengthening of Protestantism in the South, where soon the Scriptures were being used to support the slave system. Many moderate social thinkers, both Northern and Southern, also felt that only slow steps were acceptable in solving the problem of slavery.

In the wake of revivals led by itinerant preachers from Methodist and Baptist denominations and of increased preaching by blacks to blacks, the number of African Americans adhering to churches rose dramatically from the 1770s to the 1830s. During this period most Christian blacks were formally attached to white congregations, even though the informal meetings they organized for themselves often provided the deepest expression of their religion. A few African Americans were even ordained for service in largely white congregations.

The earliest and most important denomination organized by blacks for blacks was the African Methodist Episcopal Church. Its founder, Richard Allen, was born a slave and was converted by Methodists at the age of 17 while working on a Delaware plantation. He began to preach immediately, first to his family, then to his master, and then to whites and blacks in that region. Throughout his life, Allen, a person of disciplined

Richard Allen, founder of the African Methodist Episcopal (AME) Church, was a dynamo of energy, whether preaching, organizing churches, editing hymns and sermons, or negotiating with authorities for the legal rights of the AME churches.

habits himself, remained convinced that Methodism was the ideal faith for African Americans: "the plain and simple gospel [of the Methodists] suits best for any people, for the unlearned can understand, and the learned are sure to understand."

Allen taught himself to read and write, and after much labor purchased his own freedom. After working at several trades, he finally arrived in Philadelphia at the age of 26. Along with other blacks, Allen regularly attended St. George's Methodist Church in Philadelphia. Then, around 1787, a distressing incident occurred at St. George's. While Allen's friend Absalom Jones was kneeling to pray during a Sunday service, white trustees forced Jones to his feet and tried to move him out of an area reserved for whites. In response, Jones, Allen, and the other blacks left the church. About the same time, Allen and Jones founded the Free African Society, America's first self-help voluntary association for African Americans. This nondenominational society provided assistance with housing and insurance, along with spiritual encouragement, to Philadelphia's African-American community.

Despite much opposition from whites, Allen succeeded in establishing the Bethel Church for Negro Methodists in 1793. He himself was ordained in 1799, which marked official recognition for the preaching he had been doing for many years. Leading Philadelphia Methodists subsequently tried to prevent Allen and his colleagues from obtaining a clear title to their own church property. Yet in 1814 African Americans succeeded in organizing their own denomination, the African Methodist Episcopal Church (Bethel). Allen became its first bishop in 1816 and served the growing body as a beloved leader until his death in 1831.

By the time of Allen's death, other Northern blacks had also begun to organize churches for themselves. Local congregations of African-American Methodists, Baptists, and Presbyterians could be found in all major urban areas. By 1822 there were a black Episcopal association and three

Methodist denominations. Black Baptists, like their white counterparts, stressed congregational autonomy and so were slower to organize. But after many years of cooperation with white Baptist mission agencies, in 1845 blacks established the African Baptist Missionary Society.

By the 1820s, African-American ministers were becoming important leaders of the abolitionist movement. Although African-American denominations, like white ones, ordained only men, at least some black women, such as Allen's associate Jarena Lee, did work as lay preachers. In the slave South there were significantly fewer chances for blacks to organize churches and voluntary societies. Yet such institutions did come into existence. Despite the notorious "slave codes" that prohibited meetings and made it illegal to teach slaves to read, Christianity made progress. Some masters encouraged their slaves in religious activities. But even where owners forbade religious meetings, slaves were often able to meet in secret for prayer, exhortation, and preaching from fellow blacks.

At such meetings and on many other occasions, singing was an all-important part of African-American existence. Songs and hymns recounting the biblical stories of Abraham, David, Daniel, and Jesus were especially crucial. These songs offered hope for the future and encouragement to keep going in the present. Where possible, these songs were also acted out, often in the "shout," a counterclockwise, circular dance that recalled African ritual. One of the songs, as reported by a North Carolina slave in the 1830s, expressed the longing for a better day like this:

> A few more beatings of the wind and rain,
> Ere the winter will be over—
>   Glory, Hallelujah!
> Some friends has gone before me,—
> I must try to go and meet them—
>   Glory, Hallelujah! . . .
> There's a better day a coming—
> There's a better day a coming—
>   Oh, Glory, Hallelujah!

Christianity could be a source of comfort to slaves that reconciled them to their fate in bondage. But it could also fuel rebellion. In one form

Frederick Douglass on Christianity and Slavery

Frederick Douglass was born in Maryland as the son of an unknown white man and a slave mother. After a childhood of cruelty and neglect, he was taken to Baltimore to be a house slave. There he learned to read and write and, after several abortive attempts, managed to escape to the North in 1838. Douglass soon became one of the most eloquent black voices for the abolition of slavery. As a powerful speaker, writer, and editor, he often attacked ways in which religion was used to support the slave system. His Narrative of the Life of Frederick Douglass an American Slave. Written by Himself, *which was originally published in 1845, addressed the religious question head on.*

I find, since reading over the foregoing Narrative, that I have in several instances, spoken in such a tone and manner, respecting religion, as may possibly lead those unacquainted with my religious views to suppose me an opponent of all religion. . . . What I have said respecting and against religion, I mean strictly to apply to the *slaveholding religion* of this land, and with no possible reference to Christianity proper; for, between the Christianity of this land, and the Christianity of Christ, I recognize the widest possible difference—so wide, that to receive the one as good, pure, and holy, is of necessity to reject the other as bad, corrupt, and wicked. To be the friend of the one, is of necessity to be the enemy of the other. I love the pure, peaceable, and impartial Christianity of Christ: I therefore hate the corrupt, slaveholding, women-whipping, cradle-plundering, partial and hypocritical Christianity of this land. . . .

We have men-stealers for ministers, women-whippers for missionaries, and cradle-plunderers for church members. The man who wields the blood-clotted cowskin during the week fills the pulpit on Sunday and claims to be a minister of the meek

and lowly Jesus. The man who robs me of my earnings at the end of each week meets me as a class-leader on Sunday morning, to show me the way of life, and the path of salvation. He who sells my sister, for purposes of prostitution, stands forth as the pious advocate of purity. He who proclaims it a religious duty to read the Bible denies me the right of learning to read the name of the God who made me. He who is the religious advocate of marriage robs whole millions of its sacred influence, and leaves them to the ravages of wholesale pollution. The warm defender of the sacredness of the family relation is the same that scatters whole families,—sundering husbands and wives, parents and children, sisters and brothers,—leaving the hut vacant, and the hearth desolate. . . . Revivals of religion and revivals in the slave-trade go hand in hand together. . . .

Dark and terrible as this picture is, I hold it to be strictly true of the overwhelming mass of professed Christians in America. They strain at a gnat, and swallow a camel. . . . They would be shocked at the proposition of fellowshipping a *sheep*-stealer; and at the same time they hug to their communion a *man*-stealer, and brand me with being an infidel, if I find fault with them for it. . . . . "Shall I not visit for these things? saith the Lord. Shall not my soul be avenged on such a nation as this?"

or another, whether through stories and images from the Bible or hopes about the end of the world, Christian faith contributed to major slave revolts under Gabriel Prosser in Richmond, Virginia (1800), Denmark Vesey in Charleston, South Carolina (1822), and Nat Turner in Virginia (1831). Much more commonly, Christianity emboldened slaves to disobey their masters in order to meet together for worship and song, to work hard with an eye toward freedom (at least for coming generations), and even to escape.

The biblically driven religion of African Americans, however, was not the only Protestant faith to penetrate a previously unchurched group in the early decades of the new nation. Evangelists had increasing success among the white population of the South at the same time that Protestant churches were forming among blacks. For Southern whites, Protestantism had to overcome not powerlessness, but a culture of honor which featured the display of self, manly competition, sensitivity to insult, and a great fondness for the duel.

Lower-class Baptists and Methodists provided the opening wedge for active Protestantism in the South. But gradually, the religion of the powerless also became the religion of the powerful. Evangelical Protestant preaching soon won an especially wide hearing among middle- and upper-class Southern women. They found the message of forgiveness and consolation in Christ meaningful for lives where the rough realities of slave agriculture mingled with the refined aspirations of genteel society. The tragedy that resulted, however, was that the potential of a shared faith was overwhelmed by contrasting social interests. Christian slaves thought the Bible encouraged them to be free. Christian slaveholders thought the Bible authorized the slave system.

In the North, some abolitionist Protestants used Scripture as a hammer against the chains of slavery. Particularly important were texts such as Galatians 3:28, "There is neither Jew nor Greek, there is neither bond nor free, there is neither male nor female: for ye are all one in Christ Jesus." The Southern interpretation of the Bible to justify slavery also made its mark in the North, especially by showing that the Old Testament

it STEALETH a man,
ETH him, or if he
l in his hand, he
ely be put to death.
Ex. xxi. 16.
shalt not deliver
master the servant
escaped from his
nto thee: He shall
h thee, *even* among
hat place which he
ose, in one of thy
ere it liketh him
u shalt not OPPRESS
eut. xxiii. 15, 16.
a man smite the eye
rvant, or the eye of
, that it perish, he
him go free for his
e. And if he smite
an-servant's tooth,
aid-servant's tooth;
et him go free for his
ake.—*Ex.* xxi. 26,

an be just, and do
ich is lawful and
ath not oppressed
th spoiled none by
; hath executed
ment between man

Thou shalt tread upon the lion and adder; the young lion and the dragon shalt thou trample under feet.

and man, he sh
live.—*Ezekiel* x
Is not this the
have chosen? to
bands of wicked
do the heavy b
let the OPPRESSED
and that ye br
yoke.—*Isaiah* lv
Ye tithe mint,
and cummin, and
of herbs, and pas
weightier matters
judgment, mercy,
these aught ye to
and not leave th
done.—*Matthew*

Thus man devotes his f
Chains him, and tasks h
his sweat,
With stripes, that merc
ing heart,
Weeps when she sees
beast.
I would not have a sl
ground,
To carry me, to fan me
And tremble when I wa
wealth
That sinews bought a
ever earn'd.
No; dear as freedom is,
I had much rather be m
And wear the bonds, th
on him.

DECLARATION OF THE ANTI-SLAVERY CONVENTION.

ASSEMBLED IN PHILADELPHIA, DECEMBER 4, 1833.

Convention assembled in the city of Philadelphia to organize a National Anti-Society, promptly seize the opportunity to promulgate the following DECLA-N OF SENTIMENTS, as cherished by them in relation to the enslavement ixth portion of the American people.

than fifty-seven years have elapsed since a band of patriots convened in this devise measures for the deliverance of this country from a foreign yoke. The

foundations of the social compact, a complete extinction of all the relations, end and obligations of mankind, and a presumptuous transgression of all the holy ments—and that therefore they ought to be instantly abrogated.

We further believe and affirm—That all persons of colour who possess the tions which are demanded of others, ought to be admitted forthwith to the of the same privileges, and the exercise of the same prerogatives, as others—

This illustration headed a broadside pamphlet published in December 1863 that called for a national anti-slavery society. Its figures were from classical mythology (Hercules strangling the Nemean lion), but its words were from the Bible.

Israelites owned slaves and that the Apostle Paul sent a slave, Onesimus, back to his master Philemon. In response, the fiery abolitionist William Lloyd Garrison professed he would abandon the Bible if the arguments defending slavery by Scripture were held to be valid.

By the 1840s, sectional differences supported by contentious varieties of evangelical Protestantism created a national crisis. Even as Northern and Southern political leaders battled with words, the great Protestant denominations split apart over slavery. On whether a bishop could hold slaves or not, the Methodists, the country's largest denomination and one of its largest organizations of any kind, divided North and South in 1844. The next year, the Baptist's triennial missionary convention refused to appoint a slaveholder as a missionary, which led to the division of the Baptists and the formation of the Southern Baptist Convention.

Extensive Christian activity took place on both sides of the Civil War. The Christian Commission was the most important Christian organization offering practical aid and comfort among the Northern troops.

The year the Methodists divided, Thomas Crowder, himself a Methodist and a Southerner, made a grim prophecy: if the national churches could not hold together, "a civil division of this great confederation may follow . . . , and then hearts will be torn apart, master and slave arrayed against each other, brother in the Church against brother, and the North against the South—and when thus arrayed with the fiercest passions and energies of our nature brought into action against each other, civil war and far-reaching desolation must be the final results." In light of what followed, Crowder was exactly right.

The Civil War, as a consequence, was a religious war. On both sides Protestants claimed that their cause was ordained by God. But almost none of the era's active Protestants saw the tragedy as clearly as Abraham

Lincoln, who, although religious, was never the member of a church. In his Second Inaugural Address from 1865, Lincoln captured the religious anguish of the war more effectively than any spokesperson of the Protestant churches: "Both read the same Bible, and pray to the same God; and each invokes His aid against the other. It may seem strange that any men should dare to ask a just God's assistance in writing their bread from the sweat of other men's faces, but let us judge not that we be not judged."

In the end, the armies of the North defeated the armies of the South. But even after the shooting stopped, none of the Protestants conceded anything to their foes. Opponents of slavery thought they were well rid of the system. Moderates in both North and South worried about the social disruption brought on by the war. Southern blacks rejoiced at freedom but faced a very uncertain future. Southern whites refused to admit they were wrong. This strife *among* Protestants over the issues that led to the Civil War is enough to explain both why the decade of the 1860s represents the high point of Protestant influence in the United States and why it represents also the beginning of the end of Protestant domination in America.

BANNER STATE
WOMAN'S NATIONAL

Chapter 5

Times of Trial and Renewal, 1866–1918

As soon as the Civil War was over, Daniel Alexander Payne went home. Payne had been born 54 years earlier to free black parents in Charleston, South Carolina. As an 18-year-old he had established a school for his fellow African Americans in that city. But in 1835 an act of the South Carolina legislature shut the school down. Payne briefly entertained doubts about the goodness of God. Then, however, he reasoned that if a thousand years were but a day to the Lord, as the Psalms said, he too could be patient and should not despair about God's ability to bring an end to evil. So Payne went North, studied at Gettysburg Lutheran Seminary, served as pastor at an African-American Presbyterian congregation, and finally joined the African Methodist Episcopal (AME) church. Soon he was his church's leading proponent of education, and he was recognized as one of the AME's leading theologians. As might be expected, Payne spoke out when white churches or seminaries excluded blacks simply because of their race. He was just as outspoken when the reverse occurred. He was once attacked for criticizing an AME congregation that excluded a white woman from the congregation. He replied, "I believe that the pastor who could turn away from God's sanctuary any human being on account of color was not fit to have charge of a gang of dogs."

Nannie Burroughs (holding the banner) was the founder of the National Training School for Women and Girls. She was also active in the National Baptist Convention, one of the largest black Protestant denominations, which was founded after the Civil War.

When Payne returned South after the war, he exploited the new freedom of the former slaves by helping the AME set up churches all throughout the region. The fact that Payne was successful in organizing congregations for the AME marked an important change in American religion. Black churches, even in the previously slave South, were coming into their own. But many white Christians were not at all pleased to see African-American denominations set up as independent bodies in the South. A division between black and white denominations was, however, only one of many significant developments in Protestant history after the Civil War.

The most visible development was that more kinds of Christian groups were taking root in America. Most important were Roman Catholics, who were growing rapidly to become the largest body of Christians in the country. In addition, many Protestants of non-British background, especially Lutherans from Germany and Scandinavia, were arriving in the United States. By 1900 substantial numbers of Eastern Orthodox had also arrived. And soon a growing number of Americans were not connected to Christianity in any form, like Jews who began to arrive in large numbers in the 1840s.

Protestants continued to enjoy remarkable achievements and to promote a full circle of activity, but the America where Protestants were in charge of the culture was steadily passing away. The Civil War itself contributed to this change. The war stimulated large-scale industrialization, the creation of large bureaucracies in government and industry, and the movement of people from farms to cities. Protestant values had always flourished best in small towns and rural society, but now cities were creating new American cultures.

In the defeated South, Protestantism grew stronger, but at a price. In the wake of the war's economic and cultural devastation, Protestantism offered profound consolation. Yet part of what it meant for such religion to shore up a defeated people was to permit the sins of racism that almost no one in the country, North or South, seemed willing to challenge.

The Civil War may also have done grave damage to Protestants' traditional confidence in the Bible. The Scriptures were a major prop for both sides in the war, but the way in which the Bible was used established a

Many Protestants who immigrated to America tried to assimilate while keeping their native cultures alive. The Ansgar Lutheran Church in Danevang, Texas, demonstrated its loyalties in 1908 by flying both the Danish and American flags.

troubling precedent. The belief that the Bible could be perfectly accommodated to support one side, and one side only, led some people to wonder if reliance on the Bible was not just a smokescreen for expressing local prejudice. Such interpretations may have had something to do with rising academic attitudes that were beginning to question earlier reverence for the Bible. If the Bible could be used to say anything, then maybe it was time to stop treating Scripture as the word of God and begin to consider it as fully part of ordinary human history.

The Civil War also affected Protestants by the way in which it opened the West for settlement. So long as there was contention over whether new Western states could allow slavery, settlement was delayed as well as uncertain. But with the ending of slavery and the extension of federal power over the plains to the West Coast, expansion proceeded rapidly. Protestants, however, found that the influence they had exerted east of the

Mississippi simply would not extend to the West. Even before Protestants began missionary efforts in the region, a large Hispanic Catholic population already existed in the Southwest, Mormon settlements had spread over Utah and Idaho, Indian reservations (with a mixture of indigenous and Christian faiths) were in place, immigrants from Asia were entering the region bringing Asian religions with them, and traditional resistance to religion of all kinds was widespread. The American West would become home to many vigorous Protestant groups, but none of them exercised the clout that Protestant bodies exerted, well into the 20th century, over parts of the South, Midwest, and East.

The most visible religious change brought about by the Civil War took place among African Americans. Emancipation from slavery by no means brought legal equality, economic freedom, or educational opportunity. But it did bring opportunities for creating and managing churches. Black leaders like Daniel Payne and denominations like the AME took advantage of opportunities to extend their work into the South.

Even more important may have been the new churches founded by the liberated slaves themselves. In the five years after 1865, former slaves founded the Colored Methodist Episcopal Church and the Colored Cumberland Presbyterian Church as bodies separate from white oversight. Numerous Baptist associations also sprang up in the former slave states, which led eventually to the creation of state conventions and then, finally to the National Baptist Convention in 1895. The two groups that emerged from this body after a split in 1907 [the National Baptist Convention of the U.S.A., Inc., and the National Baptist Convention of America (unincorporated)] still are two of the largest denominations of black Christians in the United States.

To be sure, no single black Protestant faith existed. Even more than among American whites, self-standing, independent, often small churches have been a mainstay of black religious experience in America. A comparison between two important leaders who flourished in the generation after slavery illustrates some of the differences among them.

Booker T. Washington is known today as an educational pioneer who was willing to work within boundaries set by white society. That

A missionary preaching to the Pima Indians of Arizona in 1895. The American West proved to be the region most resistant to Protestant influence.

willingness has been praised as a tactical stroke of genius, but also condemned as an unforgivable accommodation to injustice. Washington, a lifelong Baptist, was trained at Hampton Normal and Agricultural Institute in Virginia. Throughout his life, and especially as the founder of the Tuskegee Institute in Alabama, Washington exhibited the Christian moral earnestness he had learned at Hampton. In a famous speech at Atlanta in 1895 he urged blacks to win their way in a white society through self-discipline, moral constancy, and diligence in farming and the mechanical trades. This speech has been criticized for conceding too much to the injustices of the time, but Washington was not offering self-restraint or Christian faith as a substitute for justice. Still, Washington's vision of progress was accommodating. He asked blacks to bear with injustice, to tolerate wrongs, and to proceed patiently along the path toward freedom. He defined the object of Christian faith as getting "the inner life, the heart right, and we shall then become strong where we have been weak, wise where we have been foolish."

"Oh! Come down from Heben, en ride roun' in de hearts ov des sinners": This wood engraving, published in *Frank Leslie's Illustrated Newspaper* in 1885, illustrates the religious fervor associated with some African-American Protestant gatherings.

Bishop Henry McNeal Turner pursued another way. When he became disillusioned with inner religion only, he appealed for a faith pointing simultaneously towards spiritual and social freedom. During Reconstruction, Turner worked in Georgia both to establish the AME Church and also to create a government open to all citizens. When Reconstruction failed and blacks were ousted from Georgia politics, he returned to the church full time. Yet he did not lose his political vision. He became the leading black voice against repressive decisions by the U.S. Supreme Court, and he took up the call for African colonization. His bold claim in 1896 that "God is a Negro" was meant to shock both whites and blacks into pursuing consistency between inner religious belief and justice in society. But unlike Booker T. Washington, who ended his years as a widely respected figure, Bishop Turner died in Canada an embittered observer of black life in his native country.

Probably more typical than either explicit accommodation or explicit confrontation among African Americans was personal religious action. The wide-ranging career of Amanda Berry Smith was a remarkable instance of such concerns. Shortly after the end of the Civil War, she was instructed in holiness teachings at Phoebe Palmer's Tuesday meetings in New York City. Later, through connections with the AME Church and as an independent traveling minister, she promoted holiness at camp meetings in the Atlantic states, in England, and in India and Liberia. After returning to America she moved to the Chicago area, where she set up the Amanda Smith Industrial Orphan Home.

Rapid changes for African-American Protestants were emblematic of the rapidly shifting scene for American Protestants as a whole. The change that reveals the most about the situation for the Protestants is a simple statistic. In 1870, 10 million Americans lived in towns and cities with populations of 2,500 or more. By 1930, that number had risen to nearly 70 million. The cities were places of employment for immigrants from Europe as well as vast numbers of people leaving farms and rural villages. They were also places where social services often broke down, where incredible deprivation lurked just beyond the boundaries of prosperity, and where rootlessness and alienation were becoming ways of life. The shift in population to the cities did not mean that old norms of Protestantism passed away. It did mean that considerable adjustment was required by the new environment. Growing commercial pressure, greater access to higher education, and more opportunities for contact with representatives of different religions and ethnic groups all worked in some degree to undermine the Protestant character of the national religion. Protestants were also being asked to face important intellectual challenges.

The biggest was a great and growing confidence in science. The champion of the new science, who seemed to embody everything positive in the earnest pursuit of truth, was Britain's Charles Darwin, whose *On the Origin of Species* (1859) seemed to offer a model for rigorous, critical thought of all kinds. But Darwin's science did not celebrate God's design of the natural world. Rather, he proposed that randomness, rather than God, provided the basic mechanism for the natural world.

The problem was not directly Darwin's description of evolution: gradual change in species and the emergence of new species through natural processes. Many Protestants felt it was possible to show how God could have used evolutionary processes to bring species into existence. Benjamin B. Warfield from his post at Princeton Theological Seminary in New Jersey, won a reputation as one of the country's most conservative theologians. He was, for example, known as a fierce defender of the idea that the Bible was "inerrant," or absolutely truthful in all of its statements if interpreted correctly. Yet Warfield also felt that this view of the Bible could be adjusted to theories of evolution accounting for the development of life, including even human beings. In 1888 he wrote, "I am free to say, for myself, that I do not think there is any general statement in the Bible, or any part of the account of creation, either as given in Gen[esis] 1 and 2 or elsewhere alluded to, that need be opposed to evolution."

The problem was rather that evolution as a grand idea was being used increasingly as a replacement for traditional views of God and his design of the world. In prominent universities, leaders such as the educational theorist and public philosopher John Dewey turned away from the traditional effort to promote Christianity and a better society in tandem. They embraced instead the vision of a future guided by science. Andrew Dickinson White, the founding president of Cornell University, vowed that his institution would "afford an asylum for Science—where truth shall be sought for truth's sake, where it shall not be the main purpose of the Faculty to stretch or cut sciences exactly to fit 'Revealed Religion.'"

The new learning, in other words, was disrupting the settled relationship between Protestantism and the nation's intellectual life. It began the process that eventually ended Protestant control of higher education. It opened the door to secular interpretations of life. It also opened up a possibility that had barely existed in America before the last third of the century, which was a willingness of some intellectuals to publicly question the existence of God.

Some of the shifting intellectual climate was caused by new views from Europe that treated the Bible as any other book from the ancient world. Another part was reflected in the funding of the nation's universities. Almost all of the country's original colleges had been established by Protestant churches. Now the new money of industrialists (Hopkins, Cornell, Stanford, Rockefeller, Duke, Vanderbilt) took the lead. Where clergymen had made up the vast majority of college presidents in the first half of the 19th century, their place was increasingly taken up by professional academics or businessmen.

In sum, the lot of Protestants in the half century after the Civil War was greatly changed from what had it been in the half century before. In the earlier period there were serious obstacles to overcome, but Protestant energy won the day. Now the situation was different. The tide of energy was flowing away from the churches, and Protestants had to hustle to keep up.

It would be wrong, however, to suggest that Protestants sat by passively as if there was simply nothing they could do while national life slipped out of their control. In fact, the period was filled with vigorous Protestant initiatives, although some of these created problems of their own.

Dwight Lyman Moody was in a class by himself in the promotion of spirituality. After moving from his native New England to Chicago shortly before the Civil War, Moody took an active part in the work of the Young Men's Christian Association (YMCA), one of the many voluntary associations founded as a result of the antebellum revivals. Moody eagerly assisted efforts to found Sunday schools, distribute Christian literature, and bring a general Christian influence to the growing metropolis on Lake Michigan. In 1873 he enlisted the musician and songleader Ira Sankey to accompany him on a modestly conceived preaching tour of Great Britain. When the meetings proved unexpectedly successful, Moody and Sankey become instant celebrities on both sides of the Atlantic.

When Moody and Sankey returned to the United States in 1875, they were in demand everywhere. For the next quarter century, Moody, joined often by Sankey, was the nation's most respected religious figure.

Moody was not an ordained minister. As a layman he preached a message fitting the character of his age. He was not intense like Charles

LAST WEEK

OF MESSRS.

Moody & Sankey's Services

At Opera House, Haymarket,

FOR WEEK ENDING SATURDAY, MAY 29th.

SUNDAY, 23rd, at 8 a.m., for CHRISTIAN WORKERS—Tickets at Office.
„ **at 3 p.m.,** for WOMEN only—No Tickets.
„ **at 7 p.m.**—Tickets at Office.
„ **at 9 p.m.,** MEN only—No Tickets. Doors open at 8.30.

MONDAY at Noon, PRAYER MEETING.
„ **at 3.30 p.m.,** CHILDREN'S SERVICE, by H. DRUMMOND, Esq.—No Tickets.
„ **at 8 p.m.,** PRAYER MEETING, no Tickets

TUESDAY AND **WEDNESDAY**
at Noon, PRAYER MEETING. (Wednesday at noon, Special Service for Blind. Public not admitted till 11.30.)
at 3.30 p.m., ADDRESS — All Tickets issued.
at 7 p.m., ADDRESS—Tickets at Office
at 9 p.m., for WOMEN only, for convenience of Young Women employed in Houses of Business—Tickets at Office.

THURSDAY, at Noon, PRAYER MEETING.
„ **at 3.30 p.m.,** ADDRESS, all Tickets issued
„ **at 7 p.m.,** ADDRESS—Tickets at Office.
„ **at 9 p.m.,** for MEN only—Tickets at Office.

FRIDAY, at Noon, PRAYER MEETING.
„ **at 3.30 p.m.,** ADDRESS, all Tickets issued.
„ **at 7 p.m., SPECIAL FAREWELL ADDRESS** to those who have been recently converted, or who wish to become Christians. Tickets can be obtained by such by letter only.
„ **at 9 p.m.,** MEN only—Tickets at Office of Young Men's Christian Association, 165, Aldersgate Street.

SATURDAY, at Noon, PRAYER MEETING.

T. Williams, Printer, 231, Pentonville Road, N.

Dwight L. Moody and his song leader Ira Sankey built on earlier Protestant practice by directing their message to distinct groups of potential listeners—with great success.

Finney, nor did he engage in the theatrical antics of Billy Sunday, his best-known successor. Rather, Moody tried to talk sense to his audiences about God and the need for a Savior. He dressed like a conventional businessman and spoke plainly. Moody summarized his basic Christian message as the "three R's": Ruin by Sin, Redemption by Christ, and Regeneration by the Holy Ghost. He did not expound learned theology, nor did he promote sophisticated formulas for Christian action in society. Instead, he emphasized powerful themes of Christian sentiment. In his most famous statement about his own work, Moody said, "I look upon this world as a wrecked vessel. God has given me a lifeboat and said to me, 'Moody, save all you can.'"

Moody's personal influence was extended through the important institutions he founded. These included a Bible training center for lay workers in Chicago (later the Moody Bible Institute) and a summer missions conference held near his home in Northfield, Massachusetts. From these meetings came the founding, in 1876, of the Student Volunteer Movement, a great effort that encouraged thousands of students to seek "the evangelization of the world in this generation." Moody's solution to the problems of America's growing cities was primarily preaching. But a full range of other Protestants, most of whom also approved of preaching, addressed themselves to the solution of social problems as a specifically religious duty.

Fanny Crosby, Hymnwriter for the Age

Fanny J. Crosby, though blind, became the best-known hymnwriter of her generation before her death in 1915. She was herself converted while singing Isaac Watts's hymn, "Alas, and Did My Saviour Bleed?" From her base in New York City, she wrote 8,000 hymns and religious verses. Many were included in a very popular series of books entitled Gospel Hymns, *which Ira Sankey compiled to use with Dwight L. Moody's preaching campaigns. Some of Fanny Crosby's hymns, like the ones from which the following selections are taken, remain in use in Protestant churches to this day.*

from "All the Way My Saviour Leads Me":

All the way my Saviour leads me; Oh, the fullness of his love!
Perfect rest to me is promis'd In my Father's house above.
When my spirit, cloth'd immortal, Wings its flight to realms of day,
This my song thro' endless ages: Jesus led me all the way.

from "Jesus is Tenderly Calling Thee Home":

Jesus is tenderly calling thee home—
    Calling today, calling today;
Why from the sunshine of love wilt thou roam
    Farther and farther away?
Calling to day, Calling today,
Jesus is calling, is tenderly calling today.

from "Rescue the Perishing":

Rescue the perishing, Duty demands it;
Strength for thy labor the Lord will provide;
Back to the narrow way Patiently win them;
Tell the poor wand'rer a Saviour has died.
Rescue the perishing, Care for the dying;
Jesus is merciful, Jesus will save.

Ira Sankey and Fanny Crosby were the leading hymnwriters of their era. Sankey penned such lines as "O Rock Divine, O Refuge dear, A shelter in the time of storm," while many of Crosby's hymns continue to appear in modern hymnbooks.

One of the most spectacular, and also most successful, social efforts was mounted by the Salvation Army, founded in London in the 1860s by William and Catherine Booth in order to preach and provide social services to the urban poor. Under the Booths the Salvation Army put popular entertainment to use with a vengeance. Salvation Army bands rambled through densely packed urban neighborhoods blaring away on trumpets and trombones. The organization was an early user of movies to attract a crowd. The spectacle of Christians (many of whom were pacifists) clad in sharp uniforms and organized by military rank also drew attention. The Booths' point in all this show was distinctly spiritual. They wanted to attract people whom the formal churches bypassed, such as the poor, alcoholics, and prostitutes. (The group's theology was standard Methodist fare with a strong emphasis on personal holiness.)

The Salvation Army in the United States promoted the same range of activities that it had advanced in England—provision of food, shelter, and medical assistance; vocational training; elementary schooling; internships in manufacturing and farming; visits to prisons; legal aid for the indigent; and inexpensive coal in the winter. By 1904 the organization had more than 900 stations, or corps, in the United States. It was (and remains to this day) the most comprehensive Protestant outreach ever attempted in American cities.

Better known at the time, however, was an informal movement called the Social Gospel. It existed as a loosely organized force from about 1880 to the start of the Great Depression in 1929. The strong link in the American revival tradition between personal holiness and social reform contributed greatly to the Social Gospel. So also did a newer concern for the scientific study of social problems.

Leaders of the Social Gospel like the Congregationalist Washington Gladden and the German-American Baptist Walter Rauschenbusch wanted to see Christianity applied directly to the new problems created by America's rapid economic expansion. Rauschenbusch's important book from 1907, *Christianity and the Social Crisis,* drew from his own experience as a pastor in New York City and his acquaintance with secular social reformers. Its main message, however, was to use the themes of both Old

The forthright lads and lassies of the Salvation Army in 1915. The Army's work in the United States adapted techniques for reaching city populations that founders William and Catherine Booth had originally developed in industrial London.

and New Testaments in calling for Christian concern and vigorous action on behalf of the urban poor. Although the Social Gospel is often associated with more liberal trends in theology, with the Salvation Army, its leaders were trying to solve an American dilemma—how to adapt the Protestant tradition of an earlier rural America to the changing demands of a newly industrial society.

Social concern of a different sort drove large-scale efforts to control the production and use of alcoholic beverages. The various temperance and Prohibition movements aimed, respectively, to limit and ban the use of alcohol. They were successors of antebellum movements such as the fight against slavery. In both cases Christian reformers attacked a social evil (such as slavery or drunkenness) through preaching and an appeal for government action.

Soon after the Civil War, a number of temperance advocates proposed a political party to promote their cause. A convention was held in Chicago in 1869 to decide on further action. As an indication of how progressive temperance was, this was the nation's first political convention where women participated on an equal basis with men. Yet even when this cause was much more popular than it later became, direct political action was not the answer, and the Prohibitionist Party was never a major force.

Much more successful was a moral reform agency, the Women's Christian Temperance Union (WCTU). This voluntary agency flourished under the able leadership of Frances Willard, a Methodist who, after serving as a teacher in Evanston, Illinois, became increasingly active in local and national activities of the WCTU. She urged the Prohibitionist Party to broaden its concern to the general protection of the family,and she helped Dwight Moody organize women's ministries for his urban revivals.

World War I, which began in 1914, heightened fears of social disorder. Many Americans looked at the devastation in Europe and linked it to class conflict, loss of faith in God, and the collapse of Western civilization. Against this background, the prohibition movement gained momentum. The result in 1919 was the 18th Amendment to the U.S. Constitution, which prohibited "the manufacture, sale, or transportation of intoxicating

The public prayer meeting, conducted with vigor on the city streets, was a favorite tool of the Women's Christian Temperance Union (WCTU). On issues of public health, family responsibility, and the protection of women, the WCTU was one of the most progressive social associations of its day.

liquors." Prohibition did bring improvements in the nation's health and welfare, but nothing like the utopia its promoters predicted. (In 1933 the 21st Amendment to the Constitution repealed the 18th.)

Public meetings organized by Moody and high-visibility social crusades such as the prohibition movement illustrate the great energy that Protestants still possessed at the beginning of the 20th century. At the same time, the fragmentation of Protestantism was one of the reasons that these efforts no longer represented the wave of the future. As the 20th century began, the Protestants who had acted together in the 19th century to dominate American society were beginning to fall apart in quarrels among themselves. To oversimplify, three separate groups—which can be called "Modernists," "fundamentalists," and "pietists" were beginning to emerge.

Modernists were Protestants who felt it was important to adjust Christianity to new science, new economic expansion, and new ideals of

The propensity of American Protestants to carry on their business in the public square led to considerable spoofing. A cartoonist around 1880 lampooned the singing, the Bible promoting, and the mass baptisms that sometimes accompanied revival meetings.

human progress. They believed that God was best understood as imminent; that is, as a force working within human society and within human nature. Thus, modernists were convinced that the evolving shape of modern life amounted to a revelation of God's ways with the world.

Modernism won its most important victories in centers of higher learning. Arthur Cushman McGiffert, who taught at Union Theological Seminary in New York, spoke for many of the early modernists. He had studied theology in Germany and used the new approaches he learned there to stress three things: the model of the life of Christ, the need for a scientific approach to history, and the priority of social ethics. Christianity through the ages, McGiffert held, was distorted by overemphasizing the divinity of Christ and by stressing the institutions of the formal churches.

Fundamentalists represented a counterpart to modernists. A few of them were also academics who tried to defend a traditional view of the faith through intellectual means. For example, Presbyterian scholar J. Gresham Machen, published a major polemical work in 1923 entitled *Christianity and Liberalism.* His case was that the theological changes proposed by individuals like McGiffert changed the inherited faith so radically as to make it a new religion.

Most fundamentalists, however, were not intellectuals working out careful theological positions. Instead, they responded to modernist theology by rallying ordinary believers. Mostly they favored vigorous preaching, stem-winding debate, and popular writing aimed at moving the heart more than swaying the mind. To assist these efforts there was a new theology that seemed designed for desperate times. That new theology was premillennial dispensationalism, which divided the teaching of the Bible into separate divisions, or dispensations. In each of the dispensations, God was thought to act from common principles but with different purposes. Prophecy, or the parts of the Bible forecasting future events, was very important in dispensationalism. Especially important was the attempt to see what the Bible said about the end of the world. As dispensationalists interpreted Scripture, Christ would return before establishing a 1,000-year reign of peace and righteousness called the millennium (hence a "premillennial" return). The most influential formulation of dispensational teaching appeared in 1909 when the Oxford University Press published a Bible annotated by C. I. Scofield. Scofield, a lawyer before becoming a Congregational minister, intended this edition of the Scriptures to serve as a portable guide for missionaries. But the thick web of notes and annotations in which the biblical text was embedded served as a fairly complete theology. As a multimillion copy best-seller, the impact of the Scofield Reference Bible has extended well beyond the early centers of dispensationalism to influence a wide spectrum of American Protestants. Dispensationalism, with its great stress on biblical prophecy that has not yet been fulfilled, remains a potent force in American religious life. The best-selling book of any sort published in the United States in the 1970s was a popular dispensational description of the end of the world, *The Late Great Planet Earth* by Hal Lindsey.

At the start of the 20th century, dispensational theology fueled what came to be known as a fundamentalist reaction to both modernism and the perceived decline of western Christian civilization. The fundamentals being defended included the reality of the Bible as the inspired Word of God, the incarnation of Jesus Christ as the Son of God in real human flesh, the death of Christ on the cross as a substitution for the punishment humans deserved, and the reality of a literal second-coming of Christ to the earth at the end of the age.

It took the trauma of World War I, however, to galvanize a defense of such convictions into a full-fledged ecclesiastical battle. Conflict centered among the northern Presbyterians and Baptists, although there were ripples of conflict in many other denominations. The term "fundamentalist" was coined by a Baptist editor in 1920 to designate those who wanted to defend the traditional convictions of Christianity against modern attempts to reinterpret them.

Fundamentalists and modernists fought each other vigorously over such issues. The issues under debate involoved important religious questions. But the debate itself also weakened the Protestant Church in American.

Most American Protestants were never either fundamentalists or modernists. Many remained content with the churches as inherited from the 19th century. But by the start of the 20th century, there were also growing numbers of Protestants who can be called *pietists* because they were much more concerned about intense new religious experiences than they were about denominational battles or struggles over doctrine.

A revival in the holiness teachings descended from the earlier Methodists contributed a great deal to this kind of piety. Toward the end of the 19th century this revival led to significant breakaways from the main Methodist bodies. Methodists who continued to promote the possibility of entire sanctification and who looked for a distinct second work of grace after conversion sponsored a variety of camp meetings, missions, social agencies, and independent churches. Under the leadership of Daniel Sidney Warner, the denomination now known as the Church of God

Phineas Bresee (second from right), with his associate pastor and their wives, in the "Glory Barn" in 1902. The temporary structure was used by the First Church of the Nazarene in Los Angeles during the early years of the congregation until a permanent building was erected.

(Anderson, Indiana) broke from the main denomination in 1881. Phineas F. Bresee, who had been a Methodist minister, was the first of the holiness advocates to use the name "Church of the Nazarene" when in 1895 he organized an independent congregation in Los Angeles. Others who emphasized the direct work of the Holy Spirit organized the Pentecostal Church of the Nazarene in 1907. After absorbing other groups with similar aims and after dropping the name "Pentecostal" in 1919, the Church of the Nazarene became a leading proponent of holiness teachings.

The modern holiness movement was not part of fundamentalism. Yet the themes, promoters, and expressions of the two movements soon overlapped. By the middle of the 20th century, the two movements both contributed substantially to what became known as "evangelical" Protestantism.

An even more important movement than holiness, though in many ways growing out of it, was Pentecostalism. It too was a pietist movement

The Apostolic Faith Gospel Mission on Azusa Street in Los Angeles was not an impressive building (it was torn down sometime after this 1928 photo was taken). Yet from this site began the public life of Pentecostalism, which subsequently became one of the most important religious movements in the world.

because Pentecostals at first did not usually participate in large-scale denominational activities and they mostly shunned systematic contact with the broader world.

In 1906 an abandoned Methodist church in the industrial section of Los Angeles became the cradle of this new movement. William J. Seymour, a mild-mannered black holiness preacher, founded the Apostolic Faith Gospel Mission. Soon Seymour's emphasis on the work of the Holy Spirit was a local sensation that eventually gave birth to a worldwide phenomenon. Before coming to Los Angeles, Seymour had been guided by the ministry of Charles Fox Parham, who taught that those who had been converted and who wanted to be holy should seek a baptism of "the Holy Ghost and fire"—that is, a special experience of God's very presence. With many in the Methodist and holiness traditions at the end of the 19th century, Parham placed a stronger emphasis generally on the gifts of the Spirit, including the gift of physical healing brought about by prayer. He also pioneered by teaching that a special sign of the Holy Spirit's baptism would be "speaking with other tongues."

The testimony of teenager Alice Reynolds concerning what happened in Indianapolis on Easter Sunday 1907 illustrates how "speaking in tongues" was experienced:

> The warmth of God's presence in that service deeply moved me, until there was a complete melting of the reserve that had held me back from a full surrender to God. . . . Spontaneously I rose to my feet lifting my hands with a glad note of praise, "Thank God for the baptism of the Holy Spirit; praise, O praise the Lord!" . . . As this praise came from my lips, for the first time in my life I felt the physical manifestation of God's power all through my being, and I sank to the floor. God's day of Pentecost had come to a hungry teenager. . . . In a few moments my jaws began to tremble, and the praise that was literally flooding my soul came forth in languages I had never known.

Speaking in tongues would become the most visible mark of Pentecostalism. It is a practice based on New Testament passages such as Acts 2:4, where listeners at Pentecost heard the disciples of Jesus speaking in their own languages. It also draws on the Apostle Paul's discussion in the First Epistle to the Corinthians about "speaking in a tongue," which referred to a kind of ecstatic spiritual speech. Such ecstatic speech is vocalization that sounds like gibberish to outsiders but to Pentecostals is the clear mark of the Holy Spirit baptism described in the New Testament.

The revival that began at the Apostolic Faith Gospel Mission in 1906 was marked by fervent prayer, speaking in tongues, earnest new hymns, and healing of the sick. One of its most prominent features was the full participation of women in public activities. And in an America that still took racial barriers for granted, this church was also remarkable for the striking way in which blacks and Hispanics joined whites in nightly meetings. Soon the Apostolic Faith Gospel Mission became a mecca for thousands of visitors from around the world, who often went back to their homelands proclaiming the need for a special baptism of the Holy Spirit after conversion. From a number of new alliances, networks of periodicals, and circuits of preachers and faith-healers, the Assemblies of God,

Black and white (and later Hispanic) Protestant churches have mostly continued separate existences during the 20th century. This outdoor group in New York's Harlem in 1915 illustrates the continuing appeal of revival preaching among African-American communities.

established in 1914, emerged as the most important Pentecostal denomination among Caucasians.

A number of largely African-American denominations also took shape as distinctly Pentecostal groups. The Church of God in Christ, which has become the largest of these bodies, was organized in Memphis in 1897 by C. H. Mason and Charles Price Jones. For some time, they had been urging their Baptist churches to seek an experience of God's holiness after being converted. Later, after Mason journeyed to the Apostolic Faith Gospel Mission, he accepted the Pentecostal expression of speaking in tongues as a gift of the Holy Spirit. A division then occurred with Jones and his followers, who rejected speaking in tongues. Jones and his supporters became known as the Church of Christ (Holiness) U.S.A. Under the leadership of Mason, which resembled the earlier work of Francis

Asbury among the Methodists, the Church of God in Christ expanded into most parts of the United States and to many places overseas.

Denominational concerns were not priorities in the early years of the Pentecostal movement. Later observers have noted that Pentecostalism spread most rapidly among self-disciplined, often mobile folk of the middle and lower-middle classes. But an ardent desire for the unmediated experience of the Holy Spirit was a still more common characteristic of those who became Pentecostals. Today Pentecostal churches of various types make up the fastest growing Christian movements in the world.

Modernism, fundamentalism, the holiness movement, and Pentecostalism were themselves responses, at least in part, to the shifting circumstances of a rapidly changing America. Modernists, for example, tried to adjust Christianity to the scientific ideals of the new universities. In different ways, fundamentalists, holiness advocates, and Pentecostals worked to protect personal religious faith from the corrosions of modern life. Yet at a more basic level, these were all movements of the spirit. Christian faith, in a multiplying array of forms, remained vitally important to great numbers of American Protestants in the generation surrounding the start of the 20th century, even if Protestants no longer shaped the nation as decisively as they once had done.

Chapter 6

Protestants in Modern America

The recent history of American Protestants must be told as two stories. One describes the continuing participation of Protestants in public life. The other concerns the practices of religion. The two stories always overlap. But they are not the same.

The power of public Protestants during and after World War I (1914–18) is illustrated by the lives of two prominent politicians, Woodrow Wilson and William Jennings Bryan. Wilson, the son of a southern Presbyterian minister and himself a lifelong Presbyterian layman, was leader of the United States during the war. He was twice elected President, in 1912 and 1916, in part because he projected an image of deep moral sincerity. Wilson's politics incorporated the general confidence in American democratic ideals that prevailed in the Progressive Era. Yet they also incorporated his lifelong Christian commitment. He experienced a conversion in 1873, read the Bible and prayed faithfully throughout his life, and believed that the history of the United States showed the fullest expression of Christian values in human history. In these ways Wilson was a typical Protestant. He was also, unfortunately, typical in his steadfast support of Jim Crow laws that denied full civil rights to African Americans. As the leader of the United States in World War I and afterwards, Wilson tried to promote justice among nations and

Rev. Roy W. Reading, minister of a Holiness church in Smyth County, Virginia, in the 1930s, conducts an outdoor baptism. Outdoor baptisms were becoming rarer by this time, but still could attract large crowds.

The Scopes Trial of 1925 has remained very much alive in American memory, in part because its protagonists were so memorable. Both William Jennings Bryan (seated at left), who argued the case for local control over education, and Clarence Darrow (standing with folded arms), who defended modern views of evolution, became heroes to their different constituencies.

self-determination within nations. These policies were profoundly influenced by his religious perspective.

Wilson's one-time first secretary of state, William Jennings Bryan, rode his concern for public morality into the center of great controversy in the 1920s. Like Wilson a Presbyterian layman, Bryan promoted a long list of moral causes throughout a national political career that began in the 1890s. As the Democratic candidate for President in 1896, 1900, and 1908, Bryan had emphasized the Protestant virtues of small-town America. He promoted laws to protect women and children from exploitation in factories, he appealed for the right to vote for women, and he backed economic policies to help ordinary workers and farmers. When Wilson won the presidency for the Democrats in 1912, he made Bryan his secretary of state. But in 1915 Bryan resigned when he concluded that President Wilson was needlessly pushing the country toward war with Germany. In the 1920s, Bryan became famous as a spokesman against the teaching of evolution in the public schools. In his mind the social implications of the Darwinist doctrine of "the survival of the fittest" were disastrous.

Bryan's most memorable opportunity to present his views occurred in the summer of 1925 in Dayton, Tennessee. In that small southern city a high school teacher, John Scopes, was charged with teaching his students evolution, which violated a recently passed Tennessee law. The dramatic courtroom battle that ensued pitted Bryan, who regarded opposition to evolution as a defense of society's weakest members, and the renowned trial lawyer Clarence Darrow, who saw support for evolution as a blow against hide-bound tradition. Bryan's presentation was more sophisticated than portrayed in the movie and play, *Inherit the Wind,* which was based loosely on this trial. He defended, for example, an ancient age for the earth against the fundamentalist conviction that the world was only 6,000 years old. At the end of the trial, John Scopes was convicted and ordered to pay a small fine (later overturned on a technicality). But Darrow's skill in lampooning his opponent and a national press unsympathetic to Bryan left the impression that Bryan was defending tired, outmoded opinions.

In the end, Wilson and Bryan both failed—the U.S. Senate rejected Wilson's plan for a League of Nations that he hoped would ensure world peace; Bryan died only one week after the Scopes Trial. Their defeat shows that the country at large was edging away from the Protestant standards they held dear. Protestant values were now competing against more and stronger forces in the public sphere.

By the 1930s, the public face of Protestantism was changing because of a shift in the size of American denominations. The stock market crash of 1929 and the general depression that ensued were not kind to the mainstream Protestant churches. Presbyterians, Episcopalians, Congregationalists, Methodists, Baptists

A traveling preacher from South Carolina stops his trailer in a field in Alexandria, Louisiana, 1940. Throughout American history, the initiatives of ordinary men and women have accounted for much of the dynamism of all Protestant movements.

in the North, and some of the older Reformed denominations were as troubled by the times as was the nation itself. The confident link between progress in Christian faith and progress in the nation was shaken.

By contrast, more Protestant groups that had previously existed on the fringes of American life experienced a steady, even spectacular growth. Between 1926 and 1936, the last two times the United States attempted a formal census of religious affiliation, Holiness denominations like the Church of God (Anderson, Indiana), the Church of the Nazarene, and the Christian and Missionary Alliance nearly doubled in size, while Pentecostal denominations like the Church of God (Cleveland, Tennessee), the Assemblies of God, and the Church of God in Christ doubled or even tripled in membership. Fundamentalist churches, periodicals, colleges, and traveling evangelists all experienced remarkable gains as well. In the 1930s the Southern Baptist Convention added more than 1 million members (growing to more than 5 million).

During the 1930s, while more traditional churches suffered losses, the Holiness and Pentecostal churches began to boom. This woman is dancing in the Spirit during a service at the annual general assembly of the Church of God of Prophecy, around 1930.

Charles Fuller's "Old Fashioned Revival Hour" was the most popular program on network radio during much of the 1930s and 1940s. Fuller combined music and messages from traditional revival sources with an innovative savvy about using the new medium of radio.

For many Americans, a winsome radio pioneer came to represent the new visibility of the evangelical churches. Charles E. Fuller was serving as the pastor of an independent evangelical congregation near Los Angeles in 1929 when he hit upon the idea of expanding his church's ministry by using the still-new medium of radio. For a few years he aired his program locally, but then in 1937 he took the show to the nation. Within two years "The Old-Fashioned Revival Hour" was reaching a weekly audience of about 10 million listeners over the Columbia Broadcasting System (CBS). The program's mix of folksy chatter, gospel songs, and evangelistic sermons established a pattern that many other religious broadcasts would follow in the years ahead. Fuller in 1947 also played a key role in founding a new school in Pasadena, Fuller Theological Seminary, which has gone on to become the largest interdenominational seminary in the United States.

On the East Coast, theologian Reinhold Niebuhr was gaining a different sort of following. This clergyman, who was raised in the German Evangelical Church, was a pastor in Detroit for several years around the time of World War I. His experiences at the forefront of industrial strife complicated his loyalty to the liberal theology he had embraced to that point. Out of this experience, and then through a long career as an ethicist at New York's Union Theological Seminary, Niebuhr developed a theology he called "Christian realism." Niebuhr was critical of modernists for being too optimistic about human nature. But he also rejected fundamentalism for promoting naive, simplistic interpretations of the Bible. His own position stressed the contradictory character of human life. He thought people were sinners and saints at the same time; they were inherently ego-driven but could also live for others. Niebuhr's ideas were especially popular during the crises of World War II (1939–45) and in the Cold War that followed between the Soviet Union and the United States.

During World War II almost all churches rallied behind the war effort. In the burst of prosperity that followed World War II, almost all churches expanded, especially by taking advantage of new opportunities in the suburbs that burgeoned around U.S. cities.

But even as their numbers grew, Protestants were engaged in new forms of negotiation. Some of that negotiation was among themselves. In 1950 several of the older Protestant denominations created the National Council of Churches to coordinate relations with the government, improve interchurch connections, and promote projects such as making a new translation of the Bible (the copyright for the popular Revised Standard Version is owned by the National Council of Churches). A few years earlier, in 1942, a smaller organization called the National Association of Evangelicals drew together theologically conservative groups. Informal networks, such as promotion of a Billy Graham evangelistic campaign or cooperation in the civil rights movement, probably did even more to deepen communication among traditional denominations.

Some Protestant negotiation was with American society more generally. In the 1960s the term "civil religion" would be coined to describe the kind of faith that merged loyalty to God and to the American values of progress, security, prosperity, and control. Almost all who commented on "civil religion" tied it to the Protestant heritage of white Americans. Other Protestant negotiation was with groups once considered dangerous or even demonic. The gradual spread of Protestant toleration is seen most clearly in attitudes toward Roman Catholics. After World War II considerable antagonism still remained. When President Harry Truman proposed sending a formal representative to the Vatican, the prominent

Methodist bishop G. Bromley Oxnam was steadfastly opposed. Such a move, he held, would promote an "un-American policy of a union of church and state" and, in general, damage American society. Truman withdrew the nomination.

Although harsh attitudes toward Catholics continue among a few Protestants, they began to disappear rapidly in the 1950s. The election of John F. Kennedy as the nation's first Catholic President in 1960 did a great deal to break down mutual suspicion. Even more was done by the effects of the Catholics' Second Vatican Council (1962–65), which explicitly promoted fresh contact between denominations. In the last years of the 20th century, cooperation between Catholics and Protestants took place on so many levels, and for such a variety of causes, that it is easy to forget how strong Catholic-Protestant antagonism was only a short time ago.

The religious "stars" of the postwar era were experts at showing how their faith met the needs of the era. Evangelist Billy Graham emerged as a public figure in the early 1950s by combining a distinctly spiritual message with an intentionally timely application. The Bible, as Graham preached it, opened up the way of salvation in Jesus Christ to all who would believe. But at the same time, Graham warned in sternest tones that only a turn to such a biblical message would rescue the United States in its all-or-nothing struggle with worldwide communism. This combination of religious and public concern amounted to a reinvigoration of what had once been the common Protestant stance in the United States.

From his position as minister of the Marble Collegiate Church in New York, Norman Vincent Peale preached to large congregations, was a long-time fixture on the radio, and wrote such best-selling books as *The Power of Positive Thinking*.

A softer message concerning both the soul and social adjustment came from Norman Vincent Peale, a minister of the Reformed Church of America and the long-time pastor of the Marble Collegiate Church in New York City.

From that post, he proclaimed a message combining psychological, therapeutic, and scriptural elements. Peale is best known for his book *The Power of Positive Thinking,* published in 1952 and a fixture on the *New York Times* best-seller list for three years. Its message of "positive thinking" eased the minds of many in an era stretched by fears of war with the Soviet Union as well as by unprecedented economic expansion at home.

By the 1950s, Protestant women were also contributing more directly to public life than had been customary at least since the Civil War. Catherine Wood Marshall became a best-selling author in that decade by offering a measure of realistic insight, as well as moral inspiration, in her widely read books. She was the wife, and then widow, of a prominent minister, the Scottish-born Presbyterian, Peter Marshall. Marshall was at the height of his powers as the minister of the New York Avenue Presbyterian Church in Washington, D.C., and chaplain of the United States Senate, when he was felled by a heart-attack in 1949. Catherine Marshall assembled a book of her husband's sermons, and then published a well-received biography, *A Man Called Peter.* These successes launched Marshall into a writing career that made her one of the most widely read writers of her generation. Novels, like *Christy* (1967), which drew on her childhood in rural Tennessee, as well as her work as an editor of *Guideposts* magazine (founded by Norman Vincent Peale) were for many Americans effective adaptations of Protestant values to modern life.

Another important change of the postwar era was increased opportunities for women as religious leaders. Throughout American history, women have made up a majority of the members in most Protestant churches. A few sectarian groups—Quakers, holiness churches, Pentecostals—had permitted women ministers since the 19th century. But only after World War II did the major denominations begin to ordain women for the ministry. Many of the more conservative Protestant bodies continue to limit the pastorate to men, but even these churches have developed new tasks for women, like leading Bible studies, coordinating social programs, and even leading political-actions groups. For conservatives, liberals, and those in between, the huge industry of religious publishing depends very heavily on women authors, editors, and readers.

In 1977, the Rev. Jacqueline Means (left center) of Indianapolis, Indiana, became the first woman ordained to the priesthood in the Episcopal church.

During the 1960s, the kind of religious-social consensus represented by Reinhold Niebuhr, Billy Graham, Norman Vincent Peale, and Catherine Marshall was challenged by Protestant leaders who wanted to upset the system. Martin Luther King, Jr., was the leading example. King's ability to draw on sophisticated philosophy, the pacifist social theory of Mahatma Gandhi, a deep familiarity with the Scripture, and the preaching traditions of African-American churches made him a major figure. He exasperated many moderates and conservatives, who distrusted his push for civil rights and his eventual opposition to the Vietnam War. But he also became an inspiration to millions in the United States and abroad for his willingness to seek social reform aggressively but in a spirit of Christian charity.

King's powerful public critique was a visible symbol for the coming of a new era in American life. Contention rather than consensus became the watchword. The controversies of the 1960s and 1970s—civil rights, Vietnam, changing sex roles—all enlisted Protestant church members as active participants. Never, however, did Protestants all line up on the same side.

A National Guardsman with rifle at the ready watches a Poor People's March staged by the Southern Christian Leadership Conference (SCLC) in Chicago, 1968. The march was part of a nationwide call for people of all races, religions, and economic levels to assemble in Washington, D.C., to demand economic justice.

The times of public turmoil that began in the 1960s again highlighted a contrasting fate for the Protestant denominations. In general, the older bodies that had done so much to shape American life in the 19th century struggled to adjust. For some, controversy over beliefs impeded vigorous action. The colleges and seminaries of these older, mostly Northern bodies were the centers of a generally liberal theology that stressed human capacities more than traditional views of God's loving power. To the extent that such beliefs prevailed in the older denominations, or were even thought to prevail, the churches lost credibility with some of their constituents and failed to recruit new members.

By contrast, denominations that stressed traditional beliefs about the supernatural power of God and the reliability of the Bible, or that featured the newer Pentecostal emphases on the action of the Holy Spirit, continued to expand.

The Protestant bodies whose rates of growth have exceeded (and sometimes far exceeded) general population increases are nearly all characterized by labels such as "Bible-believing," "born again," "conservative," "evangelical," "fundamentalist," "holiness," "Pentecostal," or "restorationist." They include the Assemblies of God, the Christian and Missionary Alliance, the Church of God in Christ, the Seventh-day Adventists, the Church of the Nazarene, the Salvation Army, the Baptist Bible Fellowship International, the Churches of Christ, and the Church of the Nazarene.

At the end of the 1990s, about 25 percent of Americans were affiliated with these kinds of churches, while about 15 percent were affiliated with the older denominations that used to be called the Protestant mainline. This denominational shift seems to indicate that churches providing relatively clear boundaries for belief and practice, relatively sharp affirmation of the supernatural, and relatively more demands on their members have done better in modern America than those that have not.

The shift in denominational strength was reflected also in the nature of America's missionary forces. Commissioning men and women to go out from the United States to preach the Christian message overseas began in the early 19th century. It did not escape notice then or since that the rising missionary energy of American Protestants coincided with the development of the United States as a world economic power. No snap judgments can be offered on the connection between missionary growth and national expansion. Exploitation in the name of "American Christian Civilization" certainly occurred. But so did self-sacrificing dedication to the well-being of people in other lands. Missionary activity has always been one of the most important ways that Americans found out about people, places, and things far beyond the borders of their own nation.

The major 20th-century shift in denominational strength was reflected in the size of missionary contingents. The high point of missions among the older Protestant denominations came in the 1920s, when about half of the world's 29,000 missionaries were Americans or Canadians. In 1925 there were more than 3,300 American missionaries in China alone. By the 1950s, the proportion of Christian missionaries from North America had reached two-thirds of the world total. It has subsequently declined because of the rise in missionary activity among Christians from the developing world. After about 1950, most American Protestant missionaries served

Protestant interest in missionary activity shifted in the course of the 20th century from mainline denominations to newer Pentecostal, fundamentalist, and evangelical "faith missions." H. F. Reynolds, an administrator for the Church of the Nazarene, traveled widely around the world, including this visit to India.

under independent boards established around the start of the century (like the China Inland Mission) or in the wake of World War II (like the Greater European Mission). In the 1980s, 3,000 were at work translating the Scriptures with the Wycliffe Bible Translators. In addition, large numbers of missionaries were being sponsored by the Southern Baptists, the Assemblies of God, and other conservative denominations.

This shift in mission sponsorship reflected in part the general growth of fundamentalists and evangelicals in recent American history. But it also came about through intentional activities. Since 1946, for example, the Inter-Varsity Christian Fellowship has held a missionary conference for students every three years with upwards of 20,000 young people receiving a missionary challenge at each gathering.

Missionary activity has been a constant in Protestant history, while Protestant engagement in politics has fluctuated. From the repeal of Prohibition in 1933 to the 1960s, politics registered only moderate interest among Protestants. That situation changed dramatically in the last quarter of the 20th century.

A general re-integration of religion and politics among Protestants was both illustrated and accelerated by the presidency of Jimmy Carter. When Carter was campaigning for President on the Democratic ticket in 1976, it became obvious that his private life as a Baptist Sunday School teacher in Plains, Georgia, connected at many points with his public positions. The way Carter brought religion more visibly into public view did not necessarily please his fellow Southern Baptists or other Protestants, but it was an unmistakable aspect of his presidency (1977–1981). Carter pushed religion and politics closer together than they had been since the era of Wilson and Bryan. After leaving the White House in 1981, Carter continued a course that stressed moral action, traveling around the world to monitor democratic elections in other countries and supporting the work of the Christian-sponsored organization Habitat for Humanity in providing housing for the urban poor. In these ways he expanded the practical effects of what had begun years before in Sunday school.

Habitat for Humanity has been one of the most successful social organizations operating among largely Protestant circles after World War II. Here, Episcopal clergy from the Diocese of Atlanta help raise the rafters for a new home in Carrollton, Georgia.

The Baptist minister Jerry Falwell was one of the early and best-known leaders of the "New Christian Right." Activities by Falwell and similar leaders have made religion an important factor in political decisions.

Following the heightened moral sensitivities raised in the 1960s by the civil rights movement and the Vietnam War, and in the 1970s by the example of President Carter, recent decades have been filled with Protestants eager to link Christian values with public life. If the results of such linkages often appear contradictory, it reflects the many viewpoints found among the nation's Protestants. Cornel West offered one of the most radical of such visions. As a philosopher, activist, and social critic holding various posts at Yale, Princeton, and Harvard, West has argued that a combination of Christianity and Marxism is necessary to overcome the United States' stubborn retention of oppressive white racism. His book *Prophecy Deliverance! An Afro-American Revolutionary Christianity* (1982), was a major statement of how he thought biblical themes of liberation complemented radical proposals for reform.

From the other side of the political universe, the life of Jerry Falwell shows how other Protestants combine biblical elements with right-wing politics. In 1956, Falwell founded the Thomas Road Baptist Church in Lynchburg, Virginia, which then grew to become a very large church and the home base for a number of religious and political activities. In his sermons, radio and television programs, and books, Falwell has argued that biblical religion supports conservative political action. In 1979 Falwell founded the Moral Majority as a public lobby to advance such views. It disbanded 10 years later, but not before it helped cement an important alliance: the link between many evangelical and fundamentalist white Protestants and the conservative political goals of the Republican party.

Most American Protestants do not lean as far left as Cornel West or as far right as Jerry Falwell. Many public Protestants embrace what, in conventional political terms, look like contradictions. One of the most intriguing examples of such public figures is the theologian Ronald Sider, who teaches at Eastern Seminary in Philadelphia. Sider is an Anabaptist who believes that the Scriptures demand pacifism, an equitable sharing of wealth, and the firmest restraints possible on the excesses of capitalism. His best-selling book, *Rich Christians in an Age of Hunger* (1977) challenged American believers to use their wealth for the relief of the poor around the world. Yet as a social liberal, Sider is also a theological conservative who campaigns against abortion and publicly defends the literal resurrection of Christ from the dead.

A genuinely new development among Protestants has been the dramatic growth of churches organized by the nation's newer immigrants. Within the mix of Protestant congregations, an increasingly large share is made up of these new ethnic churches. In 1996, the Gallup Poll reported that 58 percent of American adults (or about 110 million out of the country's approximately 190 million people over the age of 20) identified themselves as Protestants. Of these Protestants, about one-sixth are African Americans. In addition, the number of both Asian-American and Hispanic Protestants is each into the millions. Protestant churches established by new immigrations from Korea, China, and Southeast Asia are increasingly frequent on the West Coast and in many of the country's major cities. Hispanic Protestants make up one of the fastest-growing segments of American religion as a whole.

Another international element also contributes uniquely to recent Protestant history. The rapid spread in the West of secular habits of life has led to a situation where a few missionaries from non-Western countries have begun to arrive in North America with the intent of converting

American Protestantism displays much of the same diversity as America itself. In 1983 this Chinese-American woman was photographed outside a Nazarene Church in Los Angeles.

the pagan Westerners. One of these new missionaries worked from 1992 to 1998 in the Canadian province of Manitoba. Godfrey Mawejje and his wife Agnes served several parishes made up of native Americans, long-term Canadian residents, and new immigrants speaking French, Ukrainian, and german. As one raised in a traditional African culture, Mawejje related well to the Native Americans. As one who spoke English as a second language he communicated easily with others in the same condition. As an Anglican, he adjusted easily to expectations of the Anglican Church of Canada.

The public ministry of Godfrey Mawejje brought spiritual renewal to his North American congregations. It is useful to remember that large-scale, even international developments in religious history are always connected to the inner lives of believers and the spiritual mission of the churches. The history of Protestant spirituality in recent America is every bit as complex as Protestant participation in public life. But since it involves the inner life of believers, it is probably even more important for a history of religion.

In recent decades almost all Protestant denominations have witnessed significant efforts at renovating spiritual life on the local level. For most churches, this has led to fresh thought about the weekly worship service. Over the last 25 years, most of the denominations have also issued new hymnbooks. There have also been serious efforts at liturgical reform guided by more thorough study of the Christian past.

Far and away the most important changes in the regular worship services of Protestants, however, have come from the broadening influence of Pentecostals and charismatics. The Pentecostal churches expanded very rapidly after the beginning of the century. But in those early decades, Pentecostal concentration on the special work of the Holy Spirit made them distinctive, even odd. In the years after World War II, Pentecostal themes and Pentecostal leaders have joined the mainstream. The Assemblies of God, a majority white denomination with considerable strength among Hispanics and Korean-Americans, enrolls about 2.5 million members. Its pastors and leaders play an increasingly large role outside their own denomination. The mostly black Church of God in Christ is about twice

African Americans worship through dance and music at a Church of God in Christ congregation in Mississippi around 1974. The predominately black Church of God in Christ, with about 5.5 million members in 1998, is one of the largest American denominations of any kind.

as large as the Assemblies of God, which makes it, after the National Baptist Convention of the U.S.A., Inc., the largest of the predominately African-American denominations.

Pentecostal worship is traditionally exuberant, spontaneous, and subjective. In the early decades of the movement a great quantity of new hymns expressed the heightened emotions resulting from direct contact with the Spirit. Pentecostal patterns of worship began to have a broader impact when a pair of developments occurred after World War II. First was the rise in public meetings for healing. Evangelists William Branham and Oral Roberts were the figures best known in that "healing revival." Such preachers, all from Pentecostal backgrounds, fanned out over especially the South, Southwest, and West to promote the healing of physical ills by a special work of the Holy Spirit. Typically these preachers held large public meetings, often in tents. After singing and preaching they would make an appeal for the sick or injured to come to the front for special prayer. As lines formed, the evangelist would place hands on the suffering one, usually on the forehead, and then pray fervently for the

The Pensacola Revival at Brownsville Assembly of God

In September 1997, reporter Richard Ostling featured the Pensacola revival in a report for PBS's NewsHour *with Jim Lehrer. The following excerpts are from the program's transcript. The revival experiences described here show the flavor of modern Pentecostalism, but they also resemble in many ways countless earlier experiences of conversion and consecration in American Protestant history.*

Richard Ostling: When evangelist Steve Hill gives an altar call at the end of his sermons, he virtually commands people to come forward and repent of their sins. He's been doing so four nights a week for more than two years at the Brownsville Assembly of God, a Pentecostal church in Pensacola, Florida. . . .

Steve Hill: A lot of Americans profess to be Christians, but they're not living the life. And so they walk in this sanctuary, they hear the gospel. It's strong. We preach the same gospel Jesus preached. We preach the same gospel Paul, John the Baptist preached, to get the sin out of your life, get right with God, get holy, clean your act up. And people come by the thousands to hear that. . . .

Patrick Waters [a convert at one of the meetings]: I never went back to the bars. I never called any of my old drug suppliers from Texas, none of my old clients. And I just walked away from it. I left it. . . . I've never been happier. You know, everything I have now God has given to me. The job that I have, going to school, the friends that I have, I mean, I have friends, true friends, not people that like me because I have drugs, or like me because I have a pocketful of money. . . .

Ostling: Hill was Brownsville's guest preacher on Father's Day of 1995. He concluded by asking everyone to come and be anointed by the Holy Spirit. As he touched people in the crowd many fell. The church's own pastor, John Kilpatrick, was among them.

John Kilpatrick: We'd been praying for revival for two and a half years, and then God just showed up at the end of the service. And when I turned, it just came in like a rushin' mighty wind. And it came in about sock level from behind my legs, and it felt just like a wind and my ankles slipped. And from there, here we are, almost three years later. . . . When people come in and they're messed up, they're really messed up. It takes the power of God to set those people free. And when the power of God touches you, there's going to be some kind of reaction. But people that like church sedate and quiet and real, you know, like I said, *Home and Gardens* neat and tidy, they're not going to like that kind of revival. And so it's easy to look on at something like this that's happening and find fault with it and call it mind manipulation or emotionalism, and that kind of thing. But I've been here, friend, and it's real. Trust me, it's real.

Ostling: Brownsville has inspired a new dynamism in a neighboring mainline congregation, the Pine Forest United Methodist Church. The Methodist youth group has been praying for revival, and after visiting Hill's meetings, they introduced the Brownsville experience in their own church. Young people have especially been touched by the revival. Linda Smith is Pine Forest's Youth Director.

Linda Smith: The most dramatic changes have been one of wishing that they were different, wishing that they knew God, to knowing God, being tremendously changed almost overnight, being physically changed. We can see a difference in their appearance, their behavior, their lifestyle. Their language has changed dramatically. I believe that this generation has experienced so much in trying to survive and overcome that there is nothing that the world can offer them that could outweigh the priceless treasure they will find in Jesus Christ.

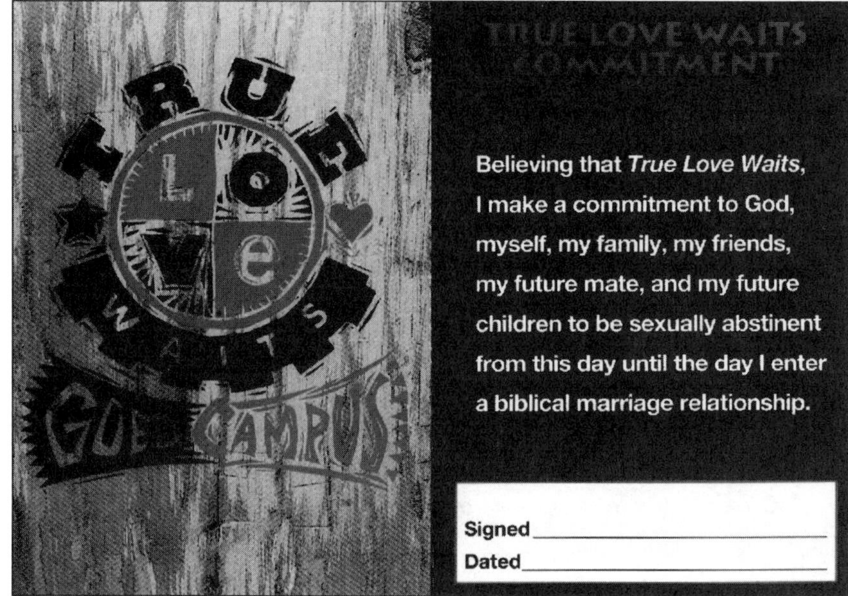

"True Love Waits" is a movement among Christian teenagers to abstain from sex until marriage. Its use of personal pledge cards is a practice picked up from earlier Protestant social movements, such as the campaigns against slavery and alcohol.

individual. Piles of discarded crutches and exuberant testimonies by the healed were widely repeated results.

The second and even more important development was the beginning of the charismatic movement in the late 1950s. This term comes from a Greek word in the New Testament meaning "gifts," referring specifically to the gifts of the Holy Spirit. The charismatic movement has promoted some of the marks of classical Pentecostalism. But it promotes them in typical American fashion by offering a spiritual smorgasbord to sample as individuals choose. Charismatic emphases include personal conversion, physical healing, speaking in tongues, participation in small group fellowships, and freshly written songs—but always as a range of open possibilities rather than formal requirements. Charismatic (in the other sense of the term) leaders have also played a major role in the charismatic movement. Since the 1970s, charismatic influences have spread into almost all of the established Protestant denominations as well as in the Roman Catholic Church.

The great changes in church music that began to take place in the 1960s were almost all related to charismatic influences. Many congregations and fellowships began to sing newly written choruses and Scripture texts set to catchy melodies. By the 1980s church musicians were exploiting a full range of pop, folk, and even rock styles as settings for this new wave of song. The increasingly common practice of singing with a combo made up of guitar, drums, and synthesizer has begun to push aside the organ as the instrument of choice in many Protestant churches. Songs projected by an overhead onto a screen have supplemented or replaced the hymnbook in many churches.

One of the most popular of the new religious choruses was written by Jack W. Hayford (b. 1934), pastor of The Church On the Way in Van Nuys, California, a congregation of the International Church of the Foursquare Gospel. That denomination was founded by the evangelist Aimee Semple McPherson (1890–1944), who combined a classical Pentecostal emphasis on healing and speaking in tongues with the kind of personal warmth that characterizes charismatic worship. From his position as a pastor, Hayford exercises a wide ministry cutting across almost all denominational boundaries. In sermons, books, and many hymns and songs, Hayford is biblical, generally evangelical, and unobtrusively charismatic. His best known song, "Majesty" is now used all around the world. It begins: "Majesty, Worship His Majesty! Unto Jesus be all glory, honor and praise."

Religious interests associated with the charismatic movement have also provided the spark for a multimillion dollar recording industry

The new megachurches often provide worship in buildings that look more like contemporary amphitheaters than traditional churches. Services at the Willow Creek Community Church in Illinois (which seats 4,650) feature Christian rock music, drama, and multimedia slide shows.

called contemporary Christian music. This industry has made stars out of singers such as Amy Grant and groups such as D. C. Talk.

The rise of "megachurches" is a development related to the charismatic movement, or at least to the relaxed institutional framework in which charismatic emphases flourish. Megachurches are spiritual shopping malls aimed at providing religious resources for people caught in the tense circumstances of modern life. The model for such congregations is the Willow Creek Community Church in South Barrington, Illinois. It began in 1975 with services in a rented movie theater as an outreach to young people and their parents. The purpose of its leaders, including founding pastor Bill Hybels, is explained on its colorful, professional Web page: "to build a church that would speak the language of our modern culture and encourage nonbelievers to investigate Christianity at their own pace, free from the traditional trappings of religion that tend to chase them away."

Within a year weekly attendance at Willow Creek was more than 1,000 and by the mid-1990s as many as 15,000 were attending weekend services on its 127-acre "campus." The Willow Creek church, complete with its 750-seat Atrium/Food Court, is hard to distinguish from the upscale corporate buildings sprinkled throughout the northwest suburbs of Chicago. The church is nontraditional in almost all its forms, but it—and at least some of its many imitators—has provided a meaningful religious message to suburbanites of the baby boom generation and their children.

Critics say that charismatic worship focuses on the self and not on God, and the megachurches cater to the transitory needs of a pleasure-driven population. They hold that modern innovations obscure the realities of human sinfulness and the holiness of God and so make it impossible to grasp the true character of divine grace.

Contemporary debate over these modern innovations resembles earlier controversy. In some sense Protestantism in America began with Puritans battling the English state church over questions of innovation, experimental spirituality, and adaptation of worship to the people. Later came similar struggles between Methodists and the original American church establishments, Protestant modernists and their opponents at the end of the 19th century, and Pentecostals and their critics in the early 20th century. The debates are important because they address the twin, but often competing, strengths of Protestantism. These strengths are a connection to the historic Christian faith and a drive to express that faith in an up-to-date, contemporary manner.

Protestant renewal in cities has not been as well publicized as the charismatic movement or the growth of megachurches, but it too has been significant in the era since World War II. The economic and social problems of urban America have made life as difficult for the churches as for other institutions. But in many of the country's largest cities, active, growing Protestant churches sustain vigorous religious life. Such churches also provide significant support for education, health care, job placement, and housing.

The Iglesia Cristiana Juan 3:16 in the Bronx, New York, is the mother church of Puerto Rican Pentecostalism in the United States. Its name in English means the Christian Church of John 3:16 ("For God so loved the world that he gave his one and only Son, that whoever believes in him shall not perish but have eternal life"). Under the leadership of the Rev. Ricardo Tañón it has engaged in many local ministries and also directed many of its members to further study and service in a wide variety of churches and religious agencies.

On the West coast, the Mount Zion Missionary Baptist Church in Los Angeles is likewise involved in feeding the hungry and developing the community. It features the fiery evangelical preaching of the Rev. E. V. Hill. Some of the dynamics involved in such churches are revealed by what appear to be the odd combination of the Rev. Hill's loyalties. He was a strong supporter of the Republican presidents Reagan and Bush (which was unusual for African-American leaders), but also helped raise money for the presidential campaigns of Jesse Jackson, and was asked by the mayor of Los Angeles to assist interracial understanding after the 1993 urban riots. These churches and many more like them face great difficulties in America's cities, but they are making a difference.

At the end of the 20th century concern for spirituality remained central for American Protestants, who have always sustained a huge appetite for devotional books. In the 19th century, countless editions of the diary of David Brainerd were snapped up. Brainerd's intense introspection while a missionary to the Delaware Indians in the 1740s became a model of religious seriousness for many of his readers. Throughout the 20th century many authors have become renowned through their writings on the spiritual life—from the books on prayer by pastor Harry Emerson Fosdick and on the consecrated life by A. B. Simpson (founder of the Christian and Missionary Alliance) at the start of the century, to a great array of authors in the last 50 years whose names are treasured in different subcommunities of the Protestant world. American Protestants have also been eager readers of spiritual writing coming from abroad, with extraordinary numbers of books becoming American best-sellers, for example, by the Scottish-born South African Oswald Chambers; Amy Carmichael, an Ulster-born missionary; or the Oxford professor C. S. Lewis.

One of the most intriguing forms of spiritual autobiography has always been the conversion narrative. In such stories written by 20th-century Protestants, there are themes both old and new. To be sure, some of the most interesting 20th-century conversion stories are those of people who left the faith. The novel *The Flight of Peter Fromm* (1973) by the mathematician Martin Gardner is one of the most interesting of such examples. The novel's central character, who seems to be Gardner's alter ego, comes from a fundamentalist background to the University of Chicago in the 1930s with the intent of converting the secular pagans to Christianity, only to be converted by them to a version of their worldview.

But the most moving accounts of conversion have always been from no religion, or merely nominal religion, to God. Many such accounts continue to be written in modern America. Ethel Walters titled her autobiography *His Eye Is on the Sparrow* (1951), which is also the name of the song by which she was best known in her lengthy public career. As one of the best-known African-American entertainers of her generation, Walters was a star of stage and screen. She was also deeply engaged with religion. From the mid-1950s she sang regularly at Billy Graham rallies (usually "His Eye Is on the Sparrow"). As a young girl Walters attended Protestant services with friends where she was particularly impressed with what she called, "oh, those hymns!" When she was 11, Walters went down to the mourner's bench at the close of such a service. There she prayed to God, and then, in her words— "it happened." She was flooded with peace and love. She wrote, "I knew I had found God." Others told her that "the light in my face electrified the whole church." For herself, Ethel Walters testified that "for always I would have an ally, a friend close by to strengthen me and cheer me on."

The conversion story of Charles Colson was different in almost every way. He was a well-connected, high-powered lawyer who eventually became a member of the White House staff of President Richard Nixon. Implicated in activities related to the Watergate scandal of 1974, Colson eventually served a seven-month jail term. Before he entered prison, however, his outlook on life was decisively altered through the witness of Tom Philips, a business executive who went out of his way to befriend Colson and to explain why he now had hope in his life. When Philips explained how attending a Billy Graham rally had helped him find "a personal relationship with God," Colson was intrigued. Philips gave Colson a copy of *Mere Christianity,* a popular book by the British literary scholar C. S. Lewis. Colson read it, pondered its message, and then also read portions from the Gospel of John that Phillips recommended.

The result was what Colson described in the title of the book he published in 1976, *Born Again.* Like many others in U.S. history, Colson was transformed when a message about trust in Christ coincided with a crisis in his own life. In Colson's case, the change was particularly dramatic, for he went from his lawyering in high places to found a ministry called Prison Fellowship, which works for the spiritual and material well-being of inmates in the United States and abroad. That movement from personal spiritual experience to outward effort at doing good is also a very common pattern in American Protestant history.

These conversion stories differ a great deal from each other. But they show that, even in the confusions of modern American life, experiences of God that resemble those of the earliest American Protestants remain extraordinarily important.

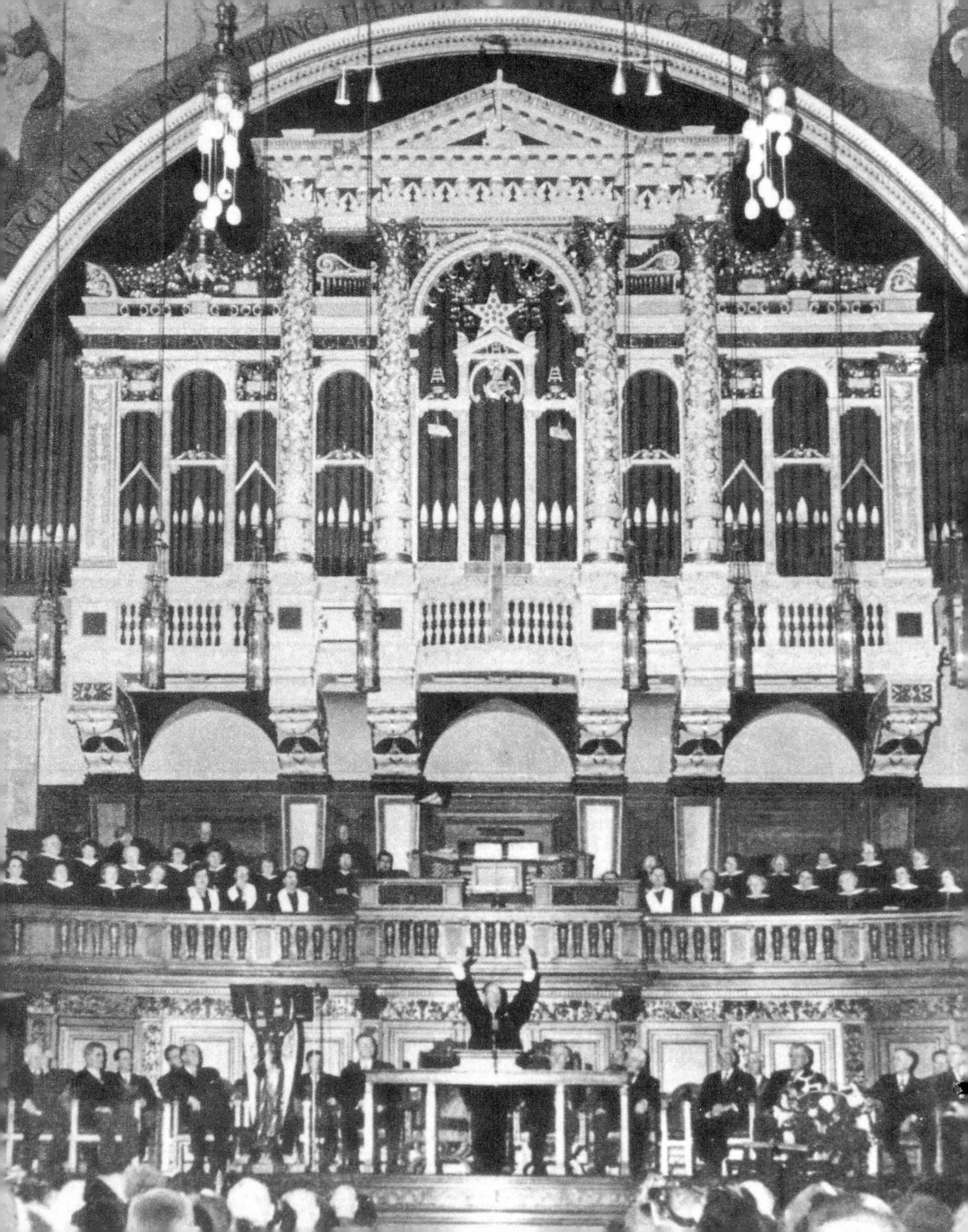

Chapter 7

Epilogue

How can anyone generalize about Protestants in America? By one recent count, there are now 19 separate Presbyterian denominations, 32 Lutheran, 36 Methodist, 37 Episcopal or Anglican, 60 Baptist, and 241 Pentecostal. But denominations are far from the only measure of Protestant diversity. The Southern Christian Leadership Conference spearheaded the civil rights movement of the 1950s and 1960s. The Christian Coalition has been a promoter of conservative politics since the early 1990s. And other voluntary societies organized by Protestants flourish beyond counting.

Attitudes and convictions are just as diverse. As only one graphic illustration, all of the major participants in the dramatic civil rights confrontations that took place in the state of Mississippi during 1964 were Protestants. They included Fannie Lou Hamer, an African-American leader of the Mississippi Freedom Democratic party, who once was sustained by thoughts of Jesus as she was being savagely beaten in the Winona, Mississippi, city jail. But they also included Sam Bowers, Imperial Wizard of the White Knights of the Ku Klux Klan, who saw himself defending the sovereignty of God and the resurrection of Jesus Christ in his conspiracy to murder three civil rights workers.

It is therefore risky to make generalizations about the history of Protestants in the United States. Nonetheless, that history can still be summarized in a number of specific observations.

American Protestant churches come in all shapes and sizes. The Tremont Temple Baptist Church in Boston, shown here in 1951, illustrates the larger and more elaborate end of the spectrum.

Region makes a big difference. Foreign visitors to the United States are regularly amazed at the great number of different churches they find. Yet the variety of churches, especially Protestant churches, pertains to the nation as a whole, not necessarily to each of its regions. America's great cities do usually provide a home for many varieties. But once outside the cities Protestants tend to be clumped fairly close together into strong regional concentrations. It has always been that way in American history. At the end of the colonial period in the 1770s, the largest Protestant denomination in the new United States was the Congregationalists, who were located almost exclusively in New England, and the second largest was the Church of England (soon to be known as Episcopalians) which was overwhelmingly concentrated in the southern colonies.

Strikingly different regional strengths remain today. The first such regional difference concerns the areas of the country as a whole. Of the four large census areas (Northeast, South, Midwest, and West), Protestants are over-represented in the South and Midwest and under-represented in the Northeast and West. That is, the percentage of Protestants in the South and Midwest is higher than the percentage of Protestants in the nation as a whole, and the reverse is true for Protestants in the Northeast and the West. Although the South has only slightly more than one-third of the nation's population, over one-half of African-American Protestants live in that region. The number of conservative, evangelical, fundamentalist, or Pentecostal Protestants is also considerably higher in the South than in the nation as a whole.

When it comes to the distribution of denominations, region also makes a very great difference. In 1990, Baptists made up the largest sector of the churched population in 14 Southern and mid-South states. Outside of the broad southern third of the country, however, Baptists are a much smaller part of the population. Lutherans are the most numerous Protestant body in Wisconsin, Iowa, Minnesota, North Dakota, South Dakota, Nebraska, and Montana. Methodists are especially strong in a band running from Delaware (the state with the highest concentration of Methodists in the country) through Nebraska. The main denominations of the Restorationist movement (Churches of Christ, Disciples of Christ, and Christian Churches) are likewise strong in the lower Midwest and upper South. There are also many counties scattered across the country where for specific historic reasons other individual denominations predominate. For example, Pentecostal churches make up the largest Protestant group in several counties in Washington, Oregon, and northern California; and there are a few counties in South Dakota where the Episcopalians are the largest denomination (because of Episcopalian missions among the Dakota Indians).

When questions are asked about Protestants in the United States, it often makes a very great difference what *part* of the country is being discussed. The United States is a big country, and the religious history of its parts is not necessarily the same as the religious history of the whole.

Race and ethnicity are important. A children's song popular in many Protestant churches emphasizes the ideal of God's love reaching out to every race:

> Jesus loves the little children of the world,
> all the children of the world,
> red and yellow, black and white,
> they are precious in his sight,
> Jesus loves the little children of the world.

The reason this song has been popular is that it expresses a profound truth of the Bible. The message of Jesus was never intended for members of only one race. Yet for the history of Protestants in the United States, race and ethnicity have always meant a very great deal.

Although it is not usually emphasized, ethnicity has been almost as important for Protestants as for Catholics. Many of the nation's earliest Protestant churches were distinctly English, as well as Anglican or Episcopalian. Immigrants from the British Isles other than England, founded distinctly Scottish or Scots-Irish Presbyterian churches, as well as distinctly Welsh Baptist, Presbyterian, and Methodist churches. Later, Lutheranism in America meant almost exclusively German or Scandinavian Lutheran. Today, Korean Presbyterians, Hispanic Pentecostals, and members of

Vietnamese Christian and Missionary Alliance churches often practice a form of Protestant faith singularly influenced by ethnic background.

The most important ethnic contribution to the history of American Protestants is African-American. Many slaveowners allowed Christianity to reach their slaves only because they thought it would make the slaves better at their tasks. Yet the Christianity that filtered through to African Americans became one of the most important contributions to American religious history. The large African-American denominations and the many noble spokespersons for Christianity among African Americans have made important contributions to general history. Even more notable was the willingness of countless slaves, freed slaves, and those threatened by slavery to find dignity, purpose, and resolution in a religion they received, ironically, from the slavemasters.

America's division of church and state is important. Protestants both helped to create and have been decisively influenced by the American separation of church and state. The decision of the government not to establish religion, or any particular denomination, was a singular innovation. At first, this decision was mostly pragmatic. In order to have a country at all, it was necessary to avoid competition among the dominant religions in the colonies.

Gradually, however, the principle that the institutions of the church and the institutions of the state should be separate became a key principle of American democracy. Almost no one in the early United States took this separation to mean the absence of religious influence on public life. But they did agree that the churches as such should be separated from the government. Sectarian Protestant bodies, particularly the Baptists, had been strong supporters of this step. In the free environment of the early United States, Baptists grew rapidly, in part because the United States had created the type of religious freedom for which they had long campaigned

American separation of church and state set the stage for several important developments. Since the denominations could no longer rely on the state for support, they were forced to compete for adherents. Competition for souls, therefore, took on a new meaning in the United States. In a competitive environment, churches and denominations that mastered the techniques of persuasion, such as Methodists, Baptists, and Restorationists, flourished. Churches and denominations that trusted in European techniques fell behind. For example, a minister's formal education (which was very important in Europe) meant far less in the new America than a minister's ability to command a crowd. One of the reason the revival became the standard American way of building up the churches was that revivals were self-produced. They did not rely on the agency of the state or a certificate of approval from some higher authority. They relied instead on the vigor, dedication, and persuasive skill of the revivalist.

The disadvantage of this way of organizing churches was a neglect of tradition and a devaluation of formal learning. The advantage was success in reaching ordinary people with the Christian message. At the very same time that European churches began to lose touch with common women and men, American churches were gaining increased loyalty from ordinary people.

Accepting the separation of church and state made many Protestants into innovators at communication. In the 18th century George Whitefield was a pioneer in the use of newspapers for publicizing his cause. The American Bible Society in the early 19th century innovated by using

Protestants have always been readers as well as churchgoers. An organization like the Church of the Nazarene's Texas Gospel Press (pictured here in about 1910), is one of thousands of publishing firms that have served American Protestants and their churches.

high-speed presses and networks of sales agents. Religious publishers were among the earliest to put advertising in their magazines. In the early 20th century, religious entrepreneurs like Paul Rader in Chicago were some of the first successful exploiters of the radio. Only with television were Protestants not at the cutting edge. That slip may be rectified with the Internet, since many Protestants of all sorts are leaping to take advantage of this new technology.

Protestants still rely much more on voluntary societies to accomplish religious and moral purposes in society than on the state. Of course the boundaries between religious influence (which has always been accepted under the Constitution) and the effort to establish a religion (which is prohibited) are contested. The modern debate over abortion on demand is a good example. Opponents of liberalized abortion laws consider their religiously based arguments to be legitimate moral persuasion, while defenders of those laws see them as illegitimate. What pro-lifers regard as the legal promotion of a religious point of view seems like the unconsitutional imposition of religious views upon government to their opponents. But even these kinds of debates are a result of the separation of church and state that Protestants helped bring about in early U.S. history.

Protestantism is connected to secularization. The term "secularization" is ambiguous. It can mean simply that certain areas of society once officially governed by churches are released from that control. (In this sense, the American separation of church and state was an example of "secularization.") But in the value laden sense in which the term is often used, it also means the withering away of real religion.

The question posed by American history is this: Did Protestant promotion of separation between church and state—along with Protestant acceptance of free markets and free interchange of ideas—actually hasten the process of secularization in this second sense?

It all depends. Considered one way, Protestants and other traditional Christians do much better in the United States at attracting and keeping adherents than do most of the European churches. Thus, since the 1920s, the percentage of Americans who claim membership in churches has risen, while percentages throughout most of the rest of the Western world have fallen. But looking at a single statistic may be deceptive. On the other side, over the same period that church membership has risen in the United States, the presence of religion as a factor in economic life, the public schools, government, and mass communications has fallen.

The Promise Keepers drew together Christian men (both Protestants and Catholics) to pray together, as at this meeting in Washington, D.C., in early October 1996. It was an unusual movement in reaching across the divide between black and white Christian believers.

Protestants, thus, may have advanced secularization, if only inadvertently. Because Protestants are so fragmented and diffuse, and because they must always be competing for adherents in the free American marketplace, they must necessarily take on the shape of the market itself. Proponents of this view concede that lots of Americans are attached to churches, but they wonder whether the content of religion in the churches is substantial. They contend that churches oriented toward spiritual consumerism may give the customers what they want, but only by diminishing the demanding, unpleasant, unflattering, and hard realities of religion.

The counter argument is that Protestantism works against secularization. In this view, fragmentation protects religious integrity. Religion adapted to local situations and shaped for the sensitivities of ordinary people has a real opportunity to connect with men and women where they are. Adapting Christianity to the mass market is therefore an assist because it shows the many ways that Christianity can speak to real-life needs and questions. In addition, voluntary activity has often strengthened the integrity of religion. A cause for which you volunteer your time, money, and energy is bound to be a cause to which you have a real commitment and which is likely to make a real difference in society.

So, has the free form of American Protestantism contributed to the secularization of American society? The best answer probably combines a yes and a no. History is not simple, and neither are the thick connections between Protestants and America's democratic society.

A great distance separates the religion of late-20th-century American Protestants from the religion of Martin Luther. That distance is geographical and chronological, but it is also conceptual. While some forms of Christianity practiced in America are closer to the religion of the Reformation than others, the gap between the 16th century and the start of the 21st century is great for all of them.

What Martin Luther would still recognize in American Protestants today is the large role played by the Bible. He would oppose violently some of the ways the Bible is interpreted, but he could see that meaningful connection with the Scriptures functions at some important place among almost all Protestants.

Luther would also recognize the importance of individual conscience as a Protestant trait descended from his willingness to stand up before the

Holy Roman Emperor and declare, "My conscience is captive to the Word of God." Again, what American Protestants do with the decisions of their consciences would not necessarily please Luther, but he could still recognize a connection.

In many other matters, Luther would be completely baffled. He would not understand the separation of church and state. He could not fathom the Protestant acceptance of modern market economies, the free trade in ideas, the prominence of self-selected leadership in the churches, the participation of women as public leaders of churches, or the reliance on religious beliefs and practices that no one in the 16th century had even imagined.

American Protestants have indeed come a great distance from Martin Luther and the age of the Reformation. To the extent that they still rely on the Bible's message of grace in Christ, however, they remain connected with the Protestant faith that began in the 16th century. To the extent that they also rely on themselves to make sense of their own religion, they show that they are likewise heirs of the Reformation. How Protestants balance this combination of reliance on Scripture and reliance on self will define their future in America, as indeed around the world.

In 1915, this men's organization of the First Methodist Church in Lancaster, Ohio, billed itself as the "largest Bible class in the world."

Appendix

Protestant Denominations

The following are Protestant churches, denominations, or associations with over 100,000 affiliates (inclusive membership) as recorded in *The Yearbook of American and Canadian Churches 2000,* ed. Eileen W. Lindner (Nashville: Abingdon, 2000).

For historical origins of the denominations, see also J. Gordon Melton, *Encyclopedia of American Religions,* 5th ed. (Detroit: Gale, 1996). The groupings are historical. In the modern era, some denominations or associations are closer in beliefs and practices to groups that do not share their historical origins than to those that do.

BRITISH BACKGROUND WITH ROOTS IN THE COLONIAL PERIOD

- American Baptist Churches in the U.S.A. (1,507,400)
- Episcopal Church (2,364,559)
- National Association of Free Will Baptists (210,461)
- Presbyterian Church (U.S.A.) (3,574,959)
- Southern Baptist Convention (15,729,356)
- Unitarian Universalist Association (191,317)
- United Church of Christ (1,421,088)
- United Methodist Church (8,400,000)

DENOMINATIONS ORIGINATING ON THE CONTINENT OF EUROPE

- Baptist General Conference [Sweden] (141,445)
- Christian Reformed Church in North America [Holland] (199,290)
- Church of the Brethren [Germany] (141,400)
- Evangelical Free Church of America [Scandinavia] (242,619)
- Evangelical Lutheran Church in America [Germany, Scandinavia] (5,178,225)
- Lutheran Church—Missouri Synod [Germany] (2,594,404)
- Reformed Church in America [Holland] (295,651)
- Wisconsin Evangelical Lutheran Synod [Germany] (411,295)

PRIMARILY AFRICAN-AMERICAN DENOMINATIONS WITH ORIGINS IN THE 19TH CENTURY

- African Methodist Episcopal Church (2,500,000)
- African Methodist Episcopal Zion Church (1,252,369)
- National Baptist Convention of America (3,500,000)

- National Baptist Convention, U.S.A., Incorporated (8,200,000)
- National Missionary Baptist Convention of America (2,500,000)
- Progressive National Baptist Convention, Inc. (2,500,000)

RESTORATIONIST CHURCHES WITH ORIGINS PRIMARILY IN THE FIRST HALF OF THE 19TH CENTURY

- Christian Congregation, Inc. (117,039)
- Christian Church, Disciples of Christ (879,436)
- Christian Churches and Churches of Christ (1,071,616)
- Churches of Christ (1,500,000)
- International Council of Community Churches (250,000)
- Reorganized Church of Jesus Christ of Latter-Day Saints (140,245)
- Seventh-day Adventist church (839,915)

HOLINESS CHURCHES WITH ORIGINS IN THE SECOND HALF OF THE 19TH CENTURY

- Christian and Missionary Alliance (345,664)
- Church of God (Anderson, Ind.) (234,311)
- Church of the Nazarene (627,054)
- Salvation Army (471,416)
- Wesleyan Church (119,914)

PENTECOSTAL DENOMINATIONS OR ASSOCIATIONS ORIGINATING IN THE 20TH CENTURY

- Assemblies of God (2,525,812)
- Church of God (Cleveland, Tenn.) (753,320)
- Church of God in Christ (5,499,875)
- Full Gospel Fellowship of Churches and Ministers International (275,200)
- International Church of the Foursquare Gospel (238,065)
- International Pentecostal Holiness Church (176,846)
- Pentecostal Assemblies of the World (1,500,000)
- Pentecostal Church of God (104,300)
- United Pentecostal Church International (500,000)

NEW DENOMINATIONS IN THE 20TH CENTURY ARISING FROM OLDER BRITISH OR COLONIAL BODIES

- American Baptist Association (275,000)
- Baptist Missionary Association of America (234,732)
- Baptist Bible Fellowship International (1,200,000)
- Conservative Baptist Association of America (200,000)
- General Association of Regular Baptist Churches (101,854)
- Presbyterian Church in America (279,549)

Chronology

1607
English settlers arrive at Jamestown, Virginia, and hold services of Anglican worship.

1619
Slaves are introduced into Virginia, and some masters eventually allow some Christian teaching for them.

1630
The main body of Puritans arrives in Massachusetts Bay from England, 10 years after a small contingent of separatist Puritans arrives in the Plymouth Colony in what is now southeastern Massachusetts.

1683
Pennsylvania is established as a proprietary colony under William Penn, who invites his fellow Quakers and many other Protestants into his colony.

1740
In the fall, George Whitefield tours New England with spectacular crowds as the high point of the colonial Great Awakening.

1754
Massachusetts minister Jonathan Edwards publishes *The Freedom of the Will*, the strongest defense of Calvinism ever written in America.

1770s
The first African-American churches are formed in South Carolina and Georgia.

1775–82
During the American Revolution, many Protestant ministers support the patriots, a few Anglicans remain loyal to Britain, and quite a few pacifists (Quakers, Mennonites, Moravians) protest warfare.

1784–89
In the wake of national independence, Methodists, Episcopalians, and Presbyterians reorganize as American denominations.

1791
The First Amendment to the U.S. Constitution prohibits the establishment of a national religion and guarantees freedom of religious practice.

1810
The American Board of Commissioners for Foreign Missions is established and soon becomes the most important early promoter of Protestant missionary work in other countries.

1816
The American Bible Society, one of the most important of the many Protestant voluntary associations of the era, is founded.

1835
An angry mob of Boston Protestants burns the Ursuline Convent (Roman Catholic) near Boston.

1844–45
The main denominations of Methodist and Baptists split into Southern and Northern halves over issues relating to slavery.

1852
Harriet Beecher Stowe's novel *Uncle Tom's Cabin* links the eradication of slavery to high religious purposes.

1859
Phoebe Palmer publishes *The Promise of the Father* as an early defense of the right of women to preach in public.

1861
The Woman's Union Missionary Society of America, a forerunner of many women's mission agencies established over the next 25 years, is founded.

1865
President Abraham Lincoln quotes several passages from the Old Testament in his Second Inaugural Address, which indicates how thoroughly the Civil War (1861–65) was a conflict between Protestants.

1867
The organization of the National Campmeeting Association for the Promotion of Christian Holiness provides a vehicle for connecting different parts of the holiness movement.

1874
Frances Willard joins the Women's Christian Temperance Union and soon transforms it into one of the most active reform agencies of the era.

1880
The Salvation Army, the Protestant denomination with the longest lasting and most successful outreach to the needs of urban America, arrives from Great Britain.

1896
Henry McNeal Turner of the African Methodist Episcopal Church publishes a controversial essay in which he claims that "God is a Negro."

1906
The modern Pentecostal movement begins with a revival at the Apostolic Faith Gospel Mission on Azusa Street in Los Angeles.

1917–18
President Woodrow Wilson, a Presbyterian, leads the United States into World War I with the intent to promote world peace defined by largely Protestant principles.

1925
At the trial of John Scopes in Dayton, Tennessee, William Jennings Bryan argues against teaching evolution in public schools, while Clarence Darrow represents the defense.

1949
Billy Graham holds a successful evangelistic campaign in Los Angeles and soon emerges as the most visible American Protestant in the world.

1950
The National Council of Churches of Christ is founded as a successor to the Federal Council of Churches and as the main ecumenical agency for mainline Protestant churches.

1950s
Mainline Protestant denominations, following the earlier example of several Holiness, Wesleyan, and Pentecostal denominations, begin to ordain women to the ministry.

1962–65
The Second Vatican Council of the Roman Catholic Church opens up a more cordial relationship between Protestants and Catholics.

1963
Rev. Martin Luther King, Jr., delivers the climactic closing address at a massive March on Washington to promote civil rights.

1974
An International Congress on World Evangelization is held in Lausanne, Switzerland, which connects many American Protestants with their associates around the world.

1995
Donald Argue, a minister of the Assemblies of God, becomes head of the National Association of Evangelicals, thereby showing how Pentecostals have entered the mainstream of American Protestant life.

1997–98
Near-daily revival services continue at a congregation of the Vineyard Movement outside Toronto and at the Brownsville Assemblies of God church in Pensecola, Florida.

1999
The Southern Baptist Convention sparks controversy by announcing a plan for extensive evangelism in connection with its annual meeting in Chicago.

Further Reading

GENERAL READING ON RELIGION IN THE UNITED STATES

Ahlstrom, Sidney. *A Religious History of the American People.* New Haven, Conn.: Yale University Press, 1972.

Butler, Jon, and Harry S. Stout, eds. *Religion in American History: A Reader.* New York: Oxford University Press, 1997.

Gaustad, Edwin S. *A Religious History of America.* Revised edition. San Francisco: Harper & Row, 1990.

Gaustad, Edwin S., and Philip L. Barlow. *New Historical Atlas of Religion in America.* 3rd ed. New York: Oxford University Press, 2000.

Keller, Rosemary Skinner, and Rosemary Radford Ruether, eds. *In Our Own Voices: Four Centuries of Women's Religious Writing.* San Francisco: HarperSanFrancisco, 1995.

Lippy, Charles H., and Peter W. Williams, ed. *Encyclopedia of the American Religious Experience.* 3 vols. New York: Scribners, 1988.

Marty, Martin. *Pilgrims in Their Own Land: 500 Years of Religion in America.* New York: Penguin, 1985.

Melton, J. Gordon, ed. *Encyclopedia of American Religion.* 6th ed. Detroit: Gale, 1999.

CHRISTIANITY IN THE UNITED STATES

Burgess, Stanley M., and Gary M. McGee, eds. *Dictionary of Pentecostal and Charismatic Movements.* Grand Rapids, Mich.: Regency, 1988.

Hatch, Nathan O., and Mark A. Noll, eds. *The Bible in America: Essays in Cultural History.* New York: Oxford University Press, 1982.

Fulop, Timothy E., and Albert J. Raboteau, eds. *African-American Religion: Interpretive Essays: History and Culture.* New York: Routledge, 1997.

Marsden, George M. *The Soul of the American University: From Protestant Establishment to Established Nonbelief.* New York: Oxford University Press, 1994.

Marty, Martin E. *Protestantism in the United States: Righteous Empire.* 2nd ed. New York: Scribners, 1986.

Noll, Mark A. *A History of Christianity in the United States and Canada.* Grand Rapids, Mich.: Eerdmans, 1992.

Reid, Daniel G., et al., eds. *Dictionary of Christianity in America.* Downers Grove, Ill.: InterVarsity Press, 1990.

Sernett, Milton C., ed. *Afro-American Religious History: A Documentary Witness.* Durham, N.C.: Duke University Press, 1985.

Wells, Ronald A., ed. *The Wars of America: Christian Views,* 2nd ed. Macon, Ga.: Mercer University Press, 1991.

EUROPEAN BACKGROUND

Bainton, Roland H. *Here I Stand: A Life of Martin Luther.* New York: Abingdon, 1950.

Barrett, David B. *World Christian Encyclopedia.* New York: Oxford University Press, 1982.

Haigh, Christopher. *English Reformations: Religion, Politics, and Society Under the Tudors.* Oxford: Clarendon Press, 1993.

Lindberg, Carter. *The European Reformations.* Cambridge, Mass.: Blackwell, 1996.

1607–1789

Curry, Thomas J. *The First Freedoms: Church and State in America to the Passage of the First Amendment.* New York: Oxford University Press, 1986.

Frey, Sylvia R., and Betty Wood. *Come Shouting to Zion: African-American Protestantism in the American South and British Caribbean to 1830.* Chapel Hill: University of North Carolina Press, 1998.

Gaustad, Edwin S. *Liberty of Conscience: Roger Williams in America.* Grand Rapids, Mich.: Eerdmans, 1991.

Hatch, Nathan O., and Harry S. Stout, eds. *Jonathan Edwards and the American Experience.* New York: Oxford University Press, 1988.

Juster, Susan. *Disorderly Women: Sexual Politics and Evangelicalism in Revolutionary New England.* Ithaca, N.Y.: Cornell University Press, 1994.

Morgan, Edmund S. *The Puritan Dilemma: The Story of John Winthrop.* Boston: Little, Brown, 1958.

Stout, Harry S. *The Divine Dramatist: George Whitefield and the Rise of Modern Evangelicalism.* Grand Rapids, Mich.: Eerdmans, 1991.

1790–1865

Bryant, Jennifer. *Lucretia Mott: A Guiding Light.* Grand Rapids, Mich.: Eerdmans, 1996.

Hambrick-Stowe, Charles E. *Charles Grandison Finney and the Rise of Modern Evangelicalism.* Grand Rapids, Mich.: Eerdmans, 1996.

Hatch, Nathan O. *The Democratization of American Christianity.* New Haven: Yale University Press, 1989.

Johnson, Curtis D. *Redeeming America: Evangelicals and the Road to Civil War.* Chicago: Ivan R. Dee, 1993.

McLoughlin, William G. *Champions of the Cherokee: Evan and John B. Jones.* Princeton: Princeton University Press, 1990.

Raboteau, Albert J. *Slave Religion: The "Invisible Institution": in the Antebellum South.* New York: Oxford University Press, 1978.

Smith, Timothy L. *Revivalism and Social Reform: American Protestantism on the Eve of the Civil War.* 2nd ed. Baltimore: Johns Hopkins University Press, 1980.

Wigger, John H. *Taking Heaven By Storm: Methodism and the Rise of Popular Christianity in America.* New York: Oxford University Press, 1998.

1866–1918

Bordin, Ruth. *Frances Willard: A Biography.* Chapel Hill: University of North Carolina Press, 1986.

Findlay, James F. *Dwight L. Moody: American Evangelist, 1837–1899.* Chicago: University of Chicago Press, 1969

Hutchison, William R. *Errand to the World: American Protestant Thought and Foreign Missions.* Chicago: University of Chicago Press, 1987.

McKinley, Edward H. *Marching to Glory: The History of the Salvation Army in the United States, 1880–1992.* 2nd ed. Grand Rapids: Eerdmans, 1995.

Marsden, George M. *Fundamentalism and American Culture: The Shaping of Twentieth-Century Evangelicalism, 1870–1925.* New York: Oxford University Press, 1980.

Sizer, Sandra S. *Gospel Hymns and Social Religion: The Rhetoric of Nineteenth-Century Revivalism.* Philadelphia: Temple University Press, 1978.

Szasz, Ferenc Morton. *The Divided Mind of Protestant America, 1880-1930.* Tuscaloosa: University of Alabama Press, 1982.

Weber, Timothy P. *Living in the Shadow of the Second Coming: American Premillennialism, 1875–1982.* Rev. ed. Chicago: University of Chicago Press, 1987.

1919–PRESENT

Balmer, Randall. *Grant Us Courage: Travels Along the Mainline of American Protestantism.* New York: Oxford University Press, 1996.

Blumhofer, Edith L. *Aimee Semple McPherson: Everybody's Sister.* Grand Rapids, Mich.: Eerdmans, 1993.

Carpenter, Joel A. *Revive Us Again: The Reawakening of American Fundamentalism.* New York: Oxford University Press, 1997.

Griffith, R. Marie. *God's Daughters: Evangelical Women and the Power of Submission.* Berkeley: University of California Press, 1997.

Harrell, David Edwin, Jr. *Oral Roberts: An American Life.* Bloomington: Indiana University Press, 1985.

Larson, Edward J. *Summer for the Gods: The Scopes Trial and American's Continuing Debate Over Science and Religion.* New York: Basic Books, 1997.

Marsh, Charles. *God's Long Summer: Stories of Faith and Civil Rights.* Princeton, N.J.: Princeton University Press, 1997.

Martin, William C. *A Prophet With Honor: The Billy Graham Story.* New York: Morrow, 1991.

Miller, Donald E. *Reconstructing American Protestantism: Christianity in the New Millennium.* Berkeley: University of California Press, 1997.

Wuthnow, Robert. *The Restructuring of American Religion: Society and Faith Since World War II.* Princeton: Princeton University Press, 1988.

Index

References to illustrations are indicated by page numbers in *italics*

Acknowledgments

I am grateful to Estelle Berger, Rachel Maxson, and Joel Moore for outstanding assistance at various stages in preparing this book. Harry Stout and Jon Butler were long-suffering and sharp-eyed editors, and the staff at Oxford University Press, especially Nancy Toff and Lisa Barnett, were helpful above and beyond the call of duty. My understanding of the breadth of American Protestant history has been greatly expanded by the many scholars who over the years have taken part in the programs of Wheaton College's Institute for the Study of American Evangelicals.

Picture Credits

Courtesy, American Antiquarian Society: 20; American Baptist Historical Society: 132; American Bible Society Archives: 68; Archives of the Billy Graham Center, Wheaton, Ill.: 13; Courtesy of the Billy Graham Center Museum, Wheaton, Ill.: 15, 32, 59, 67, 87, 94, 97; Boston Athenaeum: 69; By permission of the British Library: 31; Brown Brothers: 104; Chicago Historical Society: 92; *Chicago Tribune*: 127; Courtesy of Church of God of Prophecy International Offices, Cleveland, Tenn.: 110; Clements Library, University of Michigan: 53; © Corbis Bettman: 116; Courtesy of the Archives of the Episcopal Church, USA: 115, 119; Flower Pentecostal Heritage Center: 6, 102; Friends Historical Library of Swarthmore College: 36; Fuller Collection, Fuller Theological Seminary Archive, Pasadena, Calif.: 111; Harriet Beecher Stowe Center, Hartford, Conn.: 58, 70; The Library Company of Philadelphia: 48; Library of Congress: 12 (USZ62-111158), 18 (USZ62-35644), 19 (USZ62-39298), 22 (USZ62-90417), 25 (USZ62-75127), 35 (USZ62-5792-210316), 41 (USZ62-120506), 47 (USZ62-2583), 53, 56 (USZ62-36515-210316), 62 (USZ62-5818-210316), 63, 65, 79 (USZ62-40758-210316), 80 (USZ62-210332-B8171-7471), 82 (USZ62-106646-210316), 106 (USZ62-060671-210316), 108 (USZ62-114986-210316), 109 (USF-34-56740-D), 113 (New York World-Telegram & Sun Collection), 140-141 (USZ62-210329-126357); The Library of Virginia: 49; National Archives: 77; National Portrait Gallery, Smithsonian Institution: 51; Nazarene Archives, Kansas City, Mo.: 101, 118 (H.F. Reynolds Collection), 121 (Multi-Cultural Ministries Collection), 137 (Holiness Church of Christ Collection); Collection of The New-York Historical Society: 74; New York Public Library, Astor, Lenox and Tilden Foundations: 26 (General Research Division), 29 (Picture Collection), 98 (Picture Collection), 123 (Picture Collection); Newsweek: 120; Religious News Service: 126, 139; Courtesy of the Rhode Island Historical Society, Neg. No. Rhi (x3) 773: 44; The Salvation Army National Archives: 95; Schomburg Center for Research in Black Culture, The New York Public Library, Astor, Lenox and Tilden Foundations: 55, 88 (Photographs and Prints Division); Southern Baptist Historical Library and Archives, Nashville, Tenn.: 2, 10; The UT Institute of Texan Cultures at San Antonio: 85.

Text Credits

The sidebars in the Religion in American Life series contain extracts of historical documents. Source information on sidebars in this volume is as follows:

"A Prayer of Jonathan Edwards," p. 19: "A Sermon Preached on the Day of the Funeral of the Rev. Mr. David Brainerd" (1747), Norman Pettit, ed., *The Works of Jonathan Edwards, Vol. 7: The Life of David Brainerd* (New Haven: Yale University Press, 1985).

"The Pilgrim's Progress," p. 34: John Bunyan, *Pilgrim's Progress from this World to that which is to Come,* ed. James Blanton Wharey, 2nd ed. by Roger Sharrock (Oxford: Clarendon Press, 1960; 1st ed. 1928).

"The Voice of Anne Bradstreet," p. 40: Roger Lundin and Mark A. Noll, eds., *Voices from the Heart: Four Centuries of American Piety* (Grand Rapids, Mich.: Eerdmans, 1987).

"Frederick Douglass on Christianity and Slavery," p. 76–77: Frederick Douglass, *Narrative of the Life of Frederick Douglass, an American Slave. Written by Himself* (Boston: Anti-slavery office, 1845).

"Fanny Crosby, Hymnwriter for the Age," p. 93: Ira D. Sankey et al., *Gospel Hymns,* Nos. 1–6 (New York: Biglow and Main, 1895).

"The Pensacola Revival at Brownsville Assembly of God," pp. 124–125: "Online Focus: Religious Revival, September 10, 1997, NewsHour Transcript." [website] http://www.pbs.org/newshour/bb/religion/july-dec97/faith_9-10.html. Permission granted by the NewsHour with Jim Lehrer.

Mark A. Noll

Mark A. Noll teaches in the history department of Wheaton College, Wheaton, Illinois. His writings include general studies, including *A History of Christianity in the United States* and *Canada and Turning Points: Decisive Moments in the History of Christianity*, and he has edited or co-edited a number of books, such as *Religion and American Politics, Evangelicalism: Comparative Studies of Popular Protestantism . . . 1700–1990, Evangelicals and Science in Historical Perspective*, and *B. B. Warfield on Scripture, Science, and Evolution.*

Jon Butler

Jon Butler is the William Robertson Coe Professor of American Studies and History and Professor of Religious Studies at Yale University. He received his B.A. and Ph.D. in history from the University of Minnesota. He is the coauthor, with Harry S. Stout, of *Religion in American History: A Reader*, and the author of several other books in American religious history including *Awash in a Sea of Faith: Christianizing the American People*, which won the Beveridge Award for the best book in American history in 1990 from the American Historical Association.

Harry S. Stout

Harry S. Stout is the Jonathan Edwards Professor of American Christianity at Yale University. He is the general editor of the Religion in America series for Oxford University Press and co-editor of *Readings in American Religious History, New Directions in American Religious History, A Jonathan Edwards Reader*, and *The Dictionary of Christianity in America.* His book *The Divine Dramatist: George Whitefield and the Rise of Modern Evangelicalism* was nominated for a Pulitzer Prize in 1991.